The ULTIMATE SEARCH *Book*

U.S. Adoption, Genealogy & Other Search Secrets

by
Lori Carangelo

Genealogical Publishing Company

Baltimore, Maryland

Books by Lori Carangelo

THE ULTIMATE SEARCH BOOK
Worldwide Adoption, Genealogy & Other Search Secrets
THE ADOPTION AND DONOR CONCEPTION FACTBOOK
CHOSEN CHILDREN
Billion Dollar Babies in America's Failed
Foster Care, Adoption & Prison Systems
BLOOD RELATIVES
A True Story of Family Secrets and Murders
FACEBOOK KILLERS
KONDRO
The Untold Story of the Longview Serial Killer
PAST MISTAKES
and the Carefully Crafted Central Coast Rapist
ADOPTED KILLERS
ADOPT-A-QUOTE
Bridging the Adoption Experience-
A Collection of Feelings
8 BALL CAFÉ
True Tale of an Adoption and a Life Gone Very Wrong
NO REMORSE
FAKING CRAZY
A True Story of Adoption, Addiction, Incarceration and Acceptance
INFERTILITY CURES
ITALIAN TONIGHT!
Italian Restaurant Chefs Worldwide Share Their Recipe Secrets

Published by Genealogical Publishing Company
Baltimore, Maryland, 2015

ISBN 978-0-8063-5729-4

This book is dedicated to all who have had to endure
"impossible" searches for answers to
"Who am I?" and *"Is my child alive and well?"*

*140-million Americans Affected by Adoption and Vital Records Secrecy
(almost half the United States population)

12,000,000 Maternal Grandparents		12,000,000 Maternal Grandparents
12,000,000 Maternal Aunts & Uncles	6,000,000 Birthmothers 6,000,000 Adoptive Mothers	12,000,000 Maternal Aunts & Uncles
12,000,000 Paternal Grandparents	6,000,000 Birthfathers 6,000,000 Adoptive Fathers	12,000,000 Paternal Grandparents
12,000,00 Paternal Aunts & Uncles		12,000,000 Paternal Aunts & Uncles
7,000,000 Birth Siblings	6,000,000 Adoptees	7,000,000 Birth Siblings

    *Based upon the last National Census statistic of 315,000,000 total population if the U.S. and the Census estimate that "2.5% of the population is adopted," and taking into consideration the adoptee's two sets of parents, grandparents, aunts, uncles and siblings constituting the Mormon Family History Center's definition of "immediate family," to estimate the number of "adoption affected" Americans.

Disclaimer

The *Ultimate Search Book* has had several updated and revised editions, as an ongoing project of the author's and Americans For Open Records (AmFOR). The previous "Worldwide" print edition" includes both "how to" information as well as resources listings for every state and country, with excellent reviews from major library reference librarians (see http://AmFOR.net/UltimateSearch). This "U.S. Edition" of *The Ultimate Search Book* provides the "how to" guide for searching nationwide, revealing the ingenuity and "trade secrets" of both professional investigators and amateur "searchers" for legally circumventing roadblocks to accessing information and records wrongfully withheld, often at little or no expense.

     Mention of any particular group or individual in this book is not intended as an endorsement by the author, AmFOR, or publisher, but may be included for informational purposes for the reader to research.

     Laws, emails and website addresses (URLs) may be subject to change over time but are deemed reliable at the time of this publication. Records regarding adoptions that occurred decades ago when there were maternity homes, paper files, birth indexes, may be in paper files, books, and on microfilm, while records regarding more recent, open, semi-open, and closed adoptions may be on computers, as well as a combination of both.

     Reviews and suggestions for future editions are always welcome.

Contents

"A right is not a right in America, unless it is enjoyed by all Americans."
-Archibald Cox, Special Watergate Prosecutor

Preface

Almost everyone has someone whose absence has left a hole in their heart and may like to reconnect with them. Increasingly in the United States, there are missing children and adults whose loved ones seek answers and closure. For people who were adopted at birth or in childhood, family separation is cruelly imposed by state laws and secrecy of records intended to prevent adoptees, even in adulthood, from having knowledge of, or access to, their biological relatives so profoundly connected to their own sense of self – their very identity.

Parents have often expressed lifelong grief from loss of their children due to divorce or to an unknown fate from unjust family court interventions and "closed" adoptions. Even in "open," "semi-open" and stepparent adoptions, statutory falsification and sealing of birth records, broken promises, and unenforceable agreements can also result in grief from loss and betrayal.

The Ultimate Search Book results from 20,000 family searches and reunions in 20 years that the author and her organization, Americans For Open Records (AmFOR), helped facilitate by networking nationwide and worldwide. Over time, she became privy to "insider" search secrets of professional investigators and amateur searchers, and learned how to legally circumvent the system via public records and developed a network of sources who may be similarly motivated to interpret restrictive laws more broadly and provide the "missing pieces" – the missing knowledge and people who were lost or made to disappear -- in order to answer lifelong questions such as "Who am I? and "Is my child alive and well?"

Chapter 1:
SEARCH BASICS - 50 Search Tips for Starters

1. BEGIN WITH A LIST of all known names, dates, places related to your search. Keep notes on what you've tried to avoid duplicating your efforts. Place your list and any notes, however short, in a folder to which you can add any additional notes and documents as they are acquired.

2. LAST NAME SEARCHES: FIRST CHECK THE OBVIOUS. Sometimes the easiest or most obvious means of finding someone is overlooked. A friend of mine had always wanted to find her father who she never knew. His name was on her birth certificate along with his last known address. Within 2 minutes the online directory at http://WhitePages.com produced his current address and phone number. WhitePages.com often lists age, family members or other persons with whom they are associated, or you may find a relative with the same surname who can lead you to the person you seek. The information will only be as current as it was when posted, so if you're looking for someone who is 45 years old today and you find same name listings indicating the age is 44, or a range such as 42-45, they can be considered as a "possible." There may be links to websites such as Intellius.com or PeopleSearch.com offering listings for a fee, but with no guarantee how current.

3. REVERSE LOOKUPS, NO NAME/BIRTH DATE ONLY SEARCHES. Search Gateway, at http://searchgateway.com/ (aka page name Freeality.com) is an all-in-once search resource for name, address, phone, email, website lookups as well as Reverse Lookups PeopleFinders.com provides FREE search by name, while DOBSEARCH.com provides names of people with same date of birth, along with other helpful identifiers. (See also Search Tip #6: "YEARBOOKS FOR FIRST NAME/NO NAME SEARCHES, AND CHILD UNDER 18; and also Search Tip #25: "FIRST NAME/AGE ONLY SEARCHES.")

4. FACEBOOK. If the person you seek has an unlisted phone number not on WhitePages.com, 411.com or other online directories, and the name isn't too common, check to see if they are on Facebook. Facebook has over a billion members. By registering at http://Facebook.com, you can post information about yourself and/or about the person you seek, add photos, even a video, and maintain various levels of privacy according to your choice of settings, yet still search and contact members via their messaging option. You can also post information and photos in Newsfeeds that can be seen by friends you add, as well as their friends. Facebook pages can show you not only their names and photos but where they've been – their hometowns, schools, and affiliations, employment or business, whether they have children, their political and social interests and their Facebook friends and relatives. And in case someone is searching for you, posting names, dates and places that you have in common may help the other person find you. (See also #33-DNA TESTING/MATCHING)

5. GOOGLE SEARCH. You may "get lucky" with a Google search. Go to Google.com and try a "key words" search. First try only the name, if uncommon, to see what websites come up. If a common name such as "Johnson," use "Johnson" together with other identifiers such as birth date

and/or place. The more you know before you begin – such as accurate spelling of the first name, middle name or initial, birth date, age or age range, last known address, relatives' names, etc. – the easier it will be to whittle down same-name listings, and, of course, you can always contact all persons listed by same name if there are just a few or if they have additional identifiers in common with the person you seek It's surprising what might pop up – such as the person's own website, their genealogy, a comment they made on a chat site, a public obituary about one of their relatives, or an article written by or about the person.

6. YEARBOOKS FOR "FIRST NAME/NO NAME SEARCHES."   Do you know their date of birth and last known location?   If so, then you can guesstimate the year they graduated high school (usually the year they were 18), determine names of high schools in the area, and check the graduating classes for the year at http://Classmates.com and http://Reunions.com for people by the same first name. If you are searching for an unknown parent, adoptee, sibling or other relative, these sites may display donated high school yearbooks and you might discover the last name if you find a photo with matching first name and family resemblance.

7.   NAME CHANGE FROM MARRIAGE, DIVORCE, ADOPTION. In cases of marriage, divorce, re-marriage, and adoption, the person you seek will usually have had a name change, whether by choice or by law. While step-children in step-parent adoptions generally know who their re-married or divorced parents are, children of non-relative or stranger adoptions usually grow up not knowing who their biological parents are. In most states, even adult adoptees are not permitted to have a copy of their original (true) birth certificates, regardless whether it was an open, semi-open or closed adoption. Your adopter(s) most likely have never been given such information nor identifying documents, depending on whether they met the biological mother before the adoption, or whether the adoption was facilitated decades ago when the biological parents may have been named on certain documents. But if you were adopted and want to know about or meet your biological family, begin by asking your adopter(s) for whatever information and documents they may have – including the Petition To Adopt, Final Decree of Adoption, and your birth certificate. A checlist in Chapter 2 will explain what you can do to obtain such records from the court of jurisdiction and/or adoption agency, by state, for the state in which your adoption was finalized. Varying types of disclosure may be available to a biological parent or sibling, post-adoption. Every state now has a provision for obtaining at least non-identifying background information from both the court and agency.

8. BIRTH CERTIFICATES.   The Addendum section contains images of some of the many types of birth certificates issued in the United States, as there is no uniform document nationwide. A state may, by law, restrict who may have access to your birth certificate -- including you if you are adopted. The birth certificate is the "breeder" document establishing a person's identity in any country, and is the basis for issuance of a passport, driver's license, Social Security Card, etc. An individual may have several kinds of birth certificates issued to him. They may be Hospital Issued, County Issued; State Issued, Privately Issued, Church Issued/Baptismal, a Delayed Record, Original and, in the case of adoptees an Amended/Sealed Birth Certificate, or Foreign Birth Certificate. A birth certificate is required for a number of purposes, including to register a child in school, to obtain a Social Security Number, to obtain a driver's license, to enter the military, or to obtain a passport. In cases of stolen children and black market adoptees, the person may discover later in life that he or she has NO birth certificate.

Only a few states currently permit adult adoptees to obtain their original birth certificate simply by requesting it with ID. Chapter 2: "With or Without a Name," includes a chart that details who may contact whom and how in each state – the state in which the adoption was finalized – and also details "how to search." An adopted person's birth certificate – which will most likely be the "amended" version not available from your local vital records office, only from the central office at the state's capital - names the adopters as the parents on day of birth. But also the information may be limited depending on whether a state issues multiple forms of the same document – for instance, a "long form" birth certificate which would have the most detail, a "short form," or, as in Connecticut, a coupon sized certificate. The long form may indicate the most information, such as the hospital where the adoptee was born. The adoptee's "original" birth certificate would have been sealed (placed in a locked or restricted file) by the court when the adoption was finalized, and even if subsequently released by court order, it would only be available from the state capital office of vital records. Both the original and amended birth certificates usually bear the same Registration Number.

Although a birth certificate may be sealed (access restricted) by court order for a number of reasons, it's most often done upon finalization of an adoption via a Final Decree of Adoption – usually within one year from the Petition to Adopt and placement of the child in his adoptive home. The original record remains in the court's file for life, becoming "non-existent" in law, even if subsequently released by court order, and a new "Amended" (falsified) birth certificate is then issued which replaces the names the child's biological parents with the adopter(s) names as if they were the parent(s) on the child's date of birth. Other "identifying" information may be omitted on the Amended version, including the name of the hospital and attending physician. The date and time of birth are usually the same, unless it was a black market adoption with false original or severely altered "amended" birth certificates.

Although there are no uniform state issued birth certificates, and therefore it is difficult to spot a forgery, the United States uses a common system of state issued Birth Certificate Registration numbers as result of an agreement among the states decades ago and the adoptee's falsified version retains the same recording numbers as the original birth certificate, except that a state birth number will not appear on a birth certificate issued by a county registrar. County registrars use county registrar file numbers. A mis-match will alert a Passport Clerk to confiscate the record as fraudulent or generate a request for the original birth certificate.

THE BIRTH CERTIFICATE NUMBERING SYSTEM

Example: Birth Certificate Registration Number 1-34-75-123456:
First digit is always "1"
Next 2 digits represent State of birth: "34" is Ohio
Next 2 digits represent year of birth: "75" is 1975
Last 6 digits are the State File Number, a random sequential number

The United States is unique among nations because our birth recording system is highly decentralized and is done on many levels – hospital, county and state. In some states, authorities have attempted to make it more difficult for a "new identity" seeker to obtain state maintained birth records. But often, in these same states, other types of birth records are equally acceptable, provided they are presented in the proper context.

HOSPITAL BIRTH CERTIFICATE. Today, most people were born in hospitals but it is certainly not universal. In some states, over half of all births occurred outside hospitals. When a baby is born in a hospital, the attending physician or nurse fills out a short form indicating the time, sex and type of birth.   Once out of the recovery room, the physician completes the hospital's standard birth certificate form which will have the name and location of the hospital, the name of the attending physician and some basic information, usually provided by the mother – including the parents' names and their ages at time of the birth, the baby's name, sex and time of birth, and perhaps the parents' race and number of previous births. No two births are ever recorded at the exact same hour and minute at the same hospital, even if they occurred simultaneously, in order that the time of birth will be the ultimate identifier. At the bottom will be the signatures of the physician and witnesses and usually the hospital's own seal. A photocopy is made, notarized, and later sent to the County Recorder. The original is given to the parents.

LOCAL COUNTY ISSUED BIRTH CERTIFICATE. Upon receipt of the notarized copy from the hospital, the County Recorder will enter the birth record in the birth record book and/or computer record for that month if the county is fully automated. In some locales, the County Recorder will send a State issued birth certificate to the parents. In newborn adoptions, the Original birth certificate is withheld from the biological parents and sent together with an Amended version to the central office of Vital Records at the state capital. Years later, when the adult adoptee attempts to access his own birth certificate from county office of Vital Records, he is told he must apply only to the state Vital Records office and this is a dead giveaway to someone who may not have known he was adopted.

STATE ISSUED BIRTH CERTIFICATE. On a monthly or quarterly basis, the County Clerk forwards a listing of all births that occurred during that period to the central office of the State Vital Records office at the state capital. So for a period of some months, the newborn would not have a state issued birth certificate on file at the central state office. When the birth has been entered into the state record, the notarized photocopy of the hospital record is usually destroyed by the Country Registrar. When a newborn dies within hours or days of birth, sometimes the death certificate is recorded prior to the birth certificate. This can be either a legal occurrence or a red flag indicating a baby switch or snatch with a phony death certificate – a common occurrence in the United States and Canada in the 1950s and 1960s among physicians who sold babies for black market adoption. A directory of such baby brokers, by state, is found at http://AmFOR.net/BabyBrokers. Almost anyone born in a hospital, therefore, has at least two birth certificates, each of which has legal status, while some people never get a state issued birth certificate. The hospital issued record is their only birth certificate. Midwives who routinely deliver babies will have a supply of hospital type birth certificates and will certify the document with their own stamp or embossing tool, particularly in rural southern states, with the expectation that the parents will take the midwife supplied birth certificate to the County Registrar. But often this does not happen, so federal agencies will accept the midwife's hospital-type birth certificate. However, if someone was to present a freshly minted looking birth certificate that does not look as old as the person described in the document, it would be suspect.

PRIVATELY ISSUED FAMILY RECORD and DELAYED BIRTH CERTIFICATE. These may be incorporated into a family record book or inside a family Bible. They were and still are quite common in rural areas of the Midwest and South. Under certain circumstances, these are not acceptable as legal proof of birth. A person can obtain a state-issued Delayed Birth Certificate years later, based on these Family Records.

CHURCH ISSUED BAPTISMAL BIRTH CERTIFICATE. In areas where the Catholic, Episcopal or other church that practices baptism is strong, a signed, sealed Baptismal Birth Record is accepted as readily as one that is state-issued, even by state and federal agencies, as legal proof of birth. The information on them is whatever the parents provide. State and baptismal birth certificates may have conflicting information, so searches should aim for a "match" of other documents, newspaper birth notices, etc.

FOREIGN BIRTH CERTIFICATE. Generally, most countries maintain records of births, deaths and marriages in a central office of civil or vital records, known by different names in different languages. Church records, in addition to or in place of civil records, can be archived going back centuries and it may be easier to utilize a genealogist or website such as Ancestry.com to search records. *The Ultimate Search Book - Worldwide Edition*, is a print edition that provides information and resources for every state and country and can be obtained either direct from the publisher, Clearfield Books, or from Amazon.com or BN.com – or obtain FREE access by asking your local public or university library Acquisitions Librarian to order it:

AMENDED ADOPTION BIRTH CERTIFICATE. Prior to finalization of their adoption, adoptees have an Original birth certificate that reflects the true facts of their birth, assuming it was not a black market adoption. State laws require that, upon adoption, an Amended (legally falsified) Birth Certificate be issued which they will carry through life.

9. BIRTH INDEXES. Birth indexes are not the same as birth certificates. A birth index may cross reference mother's maiden name, father's first name, with adoptee's birth name and adoptive name. Not many birth indexes are publicly accessible any longer due to Vital Records offices learning that adoptees accessing them, as genealogists did, could discover their parents. For example, **Birth Indexes on microfilm are publicly viewable at Vital Records offices in the 5 boroughs of New York, and at your local Family History Library, but not for upstate New York.** In some states, for some years, birth indexes were purchased by genealogists and adoption searchers who sell the information.

10. INTERNATIONAL SOUNDEX REUNION REGISTRY (ISRR) is the oldest and largest free (donations only) nonprofit, voluntary registry for "next of kin" searches, whether separated by adoption or for any other reason. There are around 225,000 active registrations, at any given time. ISRR was paper based until 2003, when the volunteers began an imaging project that took five years to complete. Now all forms are digitized. ISRR was founded by the late Anthony S. Vilardi and his wife (also now deceased), Emma May Vilardi, who was an adoptee and genealogist. It is now operated by its Board of Trustees – professionals who are themselves, adoption affected. Their form for submitting information is at http://isrr.org and by mail at: ISRR, PO Box 37119, Las Vegas, NV 89137; phone number is (775) 882-7755. To achieve a "match," Soundex first emphasizes phonetic pronunciation, spelling and filing. Most of the time the input is limited to known date and time of birth, hospital and location, and the requester's name.

11. VITAL RECORDS CROSS SEARCH. Vital Records offices cross-reference women's maiden and married names. Vital Records will search records with maiden name to find a record under subsequent married name, for a fee, plus cost of the record or copies.

12. FAMILY MEMBERS AS INFORMATION SOURCE.   When searching for someone, family members, including adoptive family members, can be the quickest, easiest source of information.

13. DEPARTMENT OF MOTOR VEHICLES (DMV) – Even a non-driver may hold a DMV-issued ID Card. Depending on the state, privacy and anti-stalking laws (such as in California) now prevent DMV from disclosing an address, but some states may give an "address verification" if you can provide the name, date of birth, and last known address. This system is routinely used by auto rental agencies. An investigator using or claiming to be a car rental agent might offer a bogus address to get the actual address.

   Some DMVs may, for a fee, provide a "messaging service" or forward your letter to the person at the address that DMV has on file for their driver's license or car registration, if the name is not too common and so can be readily found. In states that still permit it, DMV may have a form for requesting the current address for a person who had a driver's license in that state.

   Many states require a person wishing to register a car to provide a Social Security Number. States that use the person's Social Security Number for their driver's license are: DC, HI, IA, IN, ID, MA, MS, MT, NV, OK and VA. A search by a woman's maiden name often produces her subsequent married name or other name change.

   In states where a driver's license does not reveal the Social Security Number, it is often recorded on DMV computers when a person receives a traffic ticket, or from auto registration filings, so a numeric search can often be run if one knows the Social Security Number.

   THESE RECORDS BELONG TO THE STATES, NOT TO THE FEDERAL GOVERNMENT, which is why access may differ from state to state. Texas is the only state that does not notify the state of the prior license that the person has obtained a Texas driver's license–so if it appears that a driver's license has long ago expired, never been renewed, and a state does not show any transfer to another state, that person may be in Texas.

   CARFAX.com, a private online company, provides a used vehicle's history for a fee, including every city and state it's been registered in, if you know the Vehicle Identification Number (VIN). A major dealership such as Ford or Chevy won't charge if you ask to "Show me the CARFAX," for one of their used vehicles while small car lots will likely charge for this.

14. LAW ENFORCEMENT can run a "Driver's License Compact" in 39 states whether or not the person has any criminal record but is simply sought for legal reasons. Law Enforcement can also search NCIS and DBA databases if the person had a prior criminal record. Sex Offender databases are publicly accessible online.

15. USPS, UPS, FEDEX.
   UNITED STATES POSTAL SERVICE (USPS) no longer provides address verification and disclosure service, but you can address a letter to the person's last known address and write "Forwarding Order Information Requested" on the envelope. You may or may not get the current address, but if the person has filed a Forwarding Order within the past year, your letter will definitely be forwarded to their current address. Or if the Forwarding Order for, for instance, Mary Jones, is most likely expired, address your letter "c/o Mary Jones or Occupant" at Mary's last known address, in which case "c/o" requires the route carrier to deliver it to whomever is at that address...and also write "Occupant: Please forward if not at this address."

UNITED PARCEL SERVICE (UPS) and FEDERAL EXPRESS (FedEx)- The "My UPS Address Book" is your own personal database for up to 2,000 shipping addresses shared with UPS.

FEDEX. A Federal Express driver can access a data bank of addresses for everyone who has ever shipped or received a package, and if addressed in error to a PO box where FedEx cannot deliver it, FedEx will automatically deliver it to a last known address while you wonder where it went.

16. SOCIAL SECURITY and THE SOCIAL SECURITY NUMBER. The Social Security Number (SSN) is a very useful piece if information. An interesting website, http://SortByName.com reveals millions of Social Security Numbers by searching with the last name, narrowed down by place or date of birth or death. It was not required that a baby's birth certificate bear a Social Security Number until the "Tax Reform Act of 1986" required parents to start putting a SSN on their tax return for children under 5. This resulted in the new practice of babies getting an SSN shortly after birth as it is now required for any "dependent" regardless of age.

The Social Security Administration no longer offers a "Locator Services" for forwarding your letter to a person whose name is not too common, along with additional identifiers and if they could be found in their database, whether dead or alive. But Social Security's Administrative Offices, which, in the past, reportedly receive only one or very few requests per month to locate a missing family member, MAY still comply with certain requests, especially if the request is accompanied by a court order or a police report of a "missing person." Like any government agency, depending on staffing, it may take awhile to hear back. A collections agency may be able to quickly track down a person's Social Security Number, which is required to access their Credit Report, and the Credit Report in turn can generate their last known and previous addresses, personal and financial information.

While it is illegal for individuals to access someone else's Social Security or Credit information, knowing their Social Security Number can provide a wealth of information about the person's background and can more positively confirm an adoptee and parent, and where the person first received their Social Security Number.

17. THE SOCIAL SECURITY NUMBERING SYSTEM
- The first 3 digits of a Social Security Number are called the "Area Number."
- Every state is assigned a different set of these numbers, so you can tell where the person resided when they first received their Social Security Card.
- 232 was transferred from West Virginia to North Carolina.
- 574, 580, 586 were assigned to Southeast Asian Refugees (from 4/75 to11/79)
- 700-728, later discontinued, had been assigned to Railroad Retirees
- The huge find-a-grave website http://SortByName.com reveals millions of Social Security Numbers with dates of birth and death, by using last name to search

SS NUMBERS ASSIGNED by State, District of Columbia, and U.S. Possessions:

416-424 Alabama	010-034 Massachusetts	408-415 Tennessee
574 Alaska	362-386 Michigan	449-467 Texas
526-527 Arizona	468-477 Minnesota	528-529 Utah
429-432 Arkansas	425-428 Mississippi	008-009 Vermont
545-573 California	486-500 Missouri	223-231 Virginia
521-524 Colorado	516-517 Montana	531-539 Washington
040-049 Connecticut	505-508 Nebraska	223-231 West Virginia
221-222 Delaware	530 Nevada	387-399 Wisconsin
577-579 District of Columbia	001-003 New Hampshire	520 Wyoming
261-267 Florida	135-158 New Jersey	
252-260 Georgia	525, 585 New Mexico	ADDITIONS:
575-576 Hawaii	050-134 New York	600-601 Arizona
518-519 Idaho	237-246 North Carolina	602-626 California
318-361 Illinois	501-502 North Dakota	589-595 Florida
303-317 Indiana	268-302 Ohio	587-588 Mississippi
478-485 Iowa	440-448 Oklahoma	585 New Mexico
509-515 Kansas	540-544 Oregon	232 North Carolina
400-407 Kentucky	159-211 Pennsylvania	U.S. POSSESSIONS:
433-439 Louisiana	035-039 Rhode Island	586 American Samoa, Guam
004-007 Maine	247-251 South Carolina	580-584 Puerto Rico
212-220 Maryland	503-504 South Dakota	580 Virgin Islands

18. THE SOCIAL SECURITY DEATH INDEX lists every deceased, non-military person who worked under or collected Social Security, and also Korean War and Vietnam War dead by name, to assist further research. It is useful for verifying whether the person you seek may be deceased and where the person last resided, which may lead you to search for living relatives in that area. The Death Index may be searched by joining Ancestry.com or at Reunions.com or via Mormon Family History Centers and public libraries. There are several genealogy websites that have versions of the Social Security Death Index which can reveal the SSN Number by searching it with name (if not too common) and date of birth.

19. CREDIT REPORTS. The largest private databases of personal information are run by Credit Bureaus. The 3 largest national Credit Bureaus are Experian (Experian.com), Trans Union (TransUnion.com) and Equifax (Equifax.com). You are entitled to one free copy of your own Credit Reports once a year (or also if you've been denied credit) via the government's website at https://www.annualcreditreport.com/ - the only site authorized by federal law for the purpose, and also directly from each of the 3 national Credit Bureaus online or by mail, but also by authorizing other companies to do so. A Credit Report may contain a wealth of information about a person, including their current and previous addresses, current and past names, date of birth, employment, credit history including types of loans, credit accounts with credit limits and balances, public records of collections, foreclosures, bankruptcy, lawsuits, wage attachments, liens and judgments, and your FICO (Fair Isaac Corporation) Score, which is calculated by the 3 national Credit Bureaus.

These databases used to be off limits to a private investigator but the federal government now allows your information to become available to an investigator. Identifiers needed to access a Credit Report include the Social Security Number, Name, Date of Birth, Address and Employment. Persons who you authorize to do so include, but are not limited to: Auto Dealerships and Retailers when applying for credit, Employers, Insurance Companies you authorize for underwriting insurance, Landlords and Real Estate Rental Agents when applying to rent property. Collection Agencies and Attorneys do not need your authorization but do need authorization from the person who has a judgment against you for money you owe. Subscriber Services such as Merlin, Choice Point, Copperstone and others can run credit reports for companies for a fee.

A common ruse of a searcher using a business name is to claim to be doing a Background Check by phone. California's law that governs background checks is somewhat different from the federal FCRA. For more information, see http://www.privacyrights.org/fs/fs16a-califbck.htm. California has a separate law that governs credit checks. (CA Civil Code §1785 et seq.)

20. INVESTIGATIVE CONSUMER REPORTS. Innovis (Innovis.com) and CoreLogic (CoreLogic.com) track and issue reports not typically found in Credit Reports, and some credit reporting agencies and investigation companies compile what is known as "investigative consumer reports." Such reports are defined under the Fair Credit Reporting Act (FCRA) as: a consumer report or portion thereof in which information on a consumer's character, general reputation, personal characteristics, or mode of living is obtained through personal interviews with neighbors, friends, or associates. An investigative consumer report is normally used in limited circumstances including employment background checks, insurance, and rental housing decisions. An investigative consumer report does not contain information about your credit record that is obtained directly from a creditor or from you.

21. ADOPTEE and PARENT SEARCHES. It is not illegal for an adoptee to search for his/her family, nor for a parent to seek his/her adult child. (See Chapter 2: "WITH OR WITHOUT A NAME" for steps to short-cut one's search.) Finding out adoption information and/or finding an unknown adoptee or parent can be attempted passively (such as posting to a registry) or actively (by utilizing search strategies).

There are usually at least two adoption files - one held by the agency or attorney, and one held by the court. Varying degrees of information can be obtained from these files by adoptees and their biological parents. It is most important to know in what state the adoption was finalized – since that state, which may be different from the state of birth, is the state that holds the records. The quickest approach for an adoptee who doesn't know, would be to simply ask his/her adopters to see the Petition to Adopt which (in older adoptions especially) may contain the names of their biological parents, and the Final Decree of Adoption which every adopter is provided by the court, and any other documents and information they may have been keeping in a safe deposit box or elsewhere.

Lacking any documents, adopters who have little or no pre-adoption information can at least share the name and location of the public (Social Services) agency branch, or private (nonprofit) agency, or attorney who handled the adoption, and in what court, i n what state and county the adoption was finalized (which is often the county in which the adopters resided at the time), and any verbal information provided by the agency or attorney at the time. Depending on how the fact of the adoption has been handled in the adoptive family, an adoptee may prefer not to ask their adopters for this information, but still has a normal need to know. Hence *The Ultimate Search Book*.

Chapter 2 contains the chart, "ADOPTION DISCLOSURE LAWS AT A GLANCE" since it is important to know what degree of disclosure might be possible in the state, from "non-identifying information" to full disclosure and contact assistance. The chapter includes "QUESTIONS FOR ADOPTEES AND PARENTS TO ASK AGENCY AND COURT." Even in the few states where adult adoptees are permitted a copy of their original birth certificates, learning how to locate unknown family members, and how to approach them when found, can seem overwhelming... and so this book goes beyond explaining "how to" search by sharing the pros and cons of search options and contact approaches under various scenarios from others' experiences and where to find support.

22. MEDICAL RECORDS. You have a right to access Medical Records in which you are named, but conditions for access is determined by State law. In California, for instance, under the Health and Safety Code Section 123110, a patient may obtain his medical records on request, in person or by mail, by signing a Release of Records. Check your state's law by Goggling or use FindLaw.com. A form may be provided by a doctor's office or hospital, but, generally, a brief letter captioned "Authorization and Release of Records," identifying the record(s) by date or approximate date and type is also sufficient. It is not required that you state a reason for the request; it is your right. You may designate that the records be sent to another doctor or other person in your behalf.

A hospital's or doctor's medical record of a birth that includes the mother's record of the delivery can provide an adoptee, or a searcher in behalf of an adoptee, with the identifying information needed to find his/her biological parents. However, if you indicate you are adopted, doors will close. It's not lying or law-breaking to omit such information.

23. LIFE OR DEATH SEARCH. It has been AmFOR's experience over the years that Judges rarely open a closed adoption record to an adoptee, even in a medical emergency such as to find a donor match for an organ transplant...or, if they do open the file and locate the biological parent, and the parent refuses contact, the Court will not inform the adoptee of the parent's identity nor identities of other biological relatives. A service available only to adoptees, called "Terminal Illness Emergency Search (TIES)," to quickly locate the biological parent(s) – see Kinsolving's website at http://reunion.adoption.com/adoption-records/medical-emergency-search.html. International Soundex Reunion Registry (ISRR) (Tip# 20) also has a "Medical Alert" service.

24. CHECKING CREDENTIALS OF DOCTORS AND HOSPITALS.

PHYSICIANS. To check physician credentials, Google the Medical Board for the state needed, and find their link for checking a physician's license. Type in the doctor's name and county where he practices. The results, (for example from the California Medical Board website), may include: If a physician has been disciplined or formally accused of wrongdoing by the Board; if a physician's practice has been temporarily restricted or suspended pursuant to a court order; if a physician has been disciplined by a medical board of another state or federal government agency, or a physician has been convicted of a felony reported to the Board after January 3, 1991; if a physician has been convicted of a misdemeanor after January 1, 2007 that results in a disciplinary action or an accusation being filed by the Board, and the accusation is not subsequently withdrawn or dismissed; if a physician has been issued a citation for a minor violation of the law by the Board within the last five years. This is not considered disciplinary action; if a physician has been issued a public letter of reprimand at time of licensure (not considered disciplinary action); any hospital disciplinary actions that resulted in the termination or revocation of the physician's privileges to provide health care services at a health care facility for a medical disciplinary cause or reason reported to the Board after January 1, 1995 (hospital disciplinary actions are not removed unless the privileges are subsequently restored); malpractice judgments and arbitration awards reported to the Board; malpractice settlements over $30,000 that meet the following criteria: Four or more in a 10-year period if the physician practices in a high-risk specialty (obstetrics, orthopedic surgery, plastic surgery and neurological surgery); 3 or more in a 10-year period if the physician practices in a low-risk specialty (all other specialties).

Information that is confidential and NOT public and would NOT appear on a record if applicable to the physician, under California law): Complaints made to the Medical Board of California; Investigations conducted by the Medical Board of California; Misdemeanor convictions that occurred after January 1, 2007 and did not result in an accusation or disciplinary action being filed by the Board; Some medical malpractice information, e.g., pending or dismissed cases. This information may be available at the local county courthouse in the "Civil Index." California Superior Court contact information.

HOSPITALS. To look up a specific hospital for licensing and accreditation, facilities, finances, patient services, the American Hospital Directory is a free service at: http://www.ahd.com/freesearch.php

PSYCHOLOGISTS, THERAPISTS, SOCIAL WORKERS. These are may be grouped under the category of Behavioral Sciences or other separate state website for looking up the status of a license, any negative background, and for complaints, etc.

25. DONOR OFFSPRING/PARENT SEARCHES and DNA TESTING. Donor conceived persons, like adopted people, express a normal desire to know about the unknown person whose genes they carry. Increasingly their anonymous donors have been wanting to know about the children they helped conceive. So Americans For Open Records (AmFOR) has provided the only totally free worldwide registry for Donor Offspring, Donor Parents, and Siblings at http://AmFOR.net/DonorOffspring. At this writing there have been 2,316 registrants and many matches. The website also provides extensive, easy to follow information, including:
• Tips for Offspring & Donors (on Searching, Posting, Connecting)
• How to Locate Using Name Search
• Affordable DNA Testing (Links)
• More Online Resources(Links)
• Fertility Doctors Who Used Own Sperm
• Articles
Suggesting to clinic staff and/or the doctor that they refer donor conceived persons and donors who inquire about confidential disclosure to AmFOR's Registry can increase matches.

26. FIRST NAME/AGE ONLY SEARCHES, AND CHILD UNDER 18. Generally, High School yearbooks on Classmates.com or at public libraries, for the year and city where the person may have graduated high school have been good resources for finding someone with only a first name, age, including adoptees and parents. By successfully matching up limited identifiers or non-identifying information with physical characteristics in yearbook photos, you then have a name (or possibly more than one "possible") to check out. For children under 18, see Chapter 2 : "WITH OR

WITHOUT A NAME" and Chapter 3: "MISSING AND RUNAWAY CHILDREN" - Usually searchers will not undertake a search for a child under age 18, especially in divorce situations, as custody orders or restraining orders may hinder the non-custodial parent's personal proximity or contact. So a searching parent concerned for their child's welfare but prevented from knowing the child's whereabouts, especially in adoption situations, might narrow down the public and private schools the child may be attending in a likely area.

If you're uncertain about the grade level for the known age of a child, ask the school board office, without mentioning that you're searching for your child. If you must state a reason, it is sufficient to indicate that you are looking at homes for sale and would like to be near a school that accommodates a child of the specific age.

27. MISSING ADULTS. Always notify Law Enforcement when you have reason to believe an adult is missing. And have available a photo of the person with their detailed description, and a list that includes their close friends and relatives, employer, and places they frequent on a regular basis such as clubs gyms, social groups etc. (which can turn up someone who witnessed the person having been last seen at a specific location). Before expanding your search, phone those most likely to know of the person's whereabouts – to verify that the person hasn't simply lost track of time while visiting with that person. If these preliminary actions don't turn up the missing person, see Chapter 4: MISSING ADULTS, for steps you can take to locate a missing adult.

28. CITY, COUNTY, STATE and COURTHOUSE PUBLIC RECORDS can be viewed free, even borrowed free in some locales depending whether they are paper records or on computer, or faxed or mailed for a fee. Public records include "vital records" -- birth, death, marriage and divorce records (except birth records of adoptees or others that may be sealed by a court); property and property tax records; business licenses; civil case information; traffic citations and certain criminal case information, etc., but cases involving children in family court, juvenile court, and probate court are confidential.

29. BETTER BUSINESS BUREAUS. BBBs serve businesses through BBB accreditation and serve consumers who may file complaints about a business's practices and determine the trustworthiness of the business via BBB's local websites

30. IF YOU ARE DENIED ACCESS TO RECORDS. Most records of the Court and Vital Records offices are intended to be "public records" but clerks may refuse access to some to which you are ordinarily permitted access. You are also entitled to Police Reports in which you are named or that are related to a matter for which you are charged with a crime. Witness statements may have witness names blocked (blackened) for the witness' protection. Rape victims' reports may be confidential. If you are denied access or a copy, you will need to phone the local Bar Association or State Attorney's office, or provide the clerk or his/her supervisor with your written Freedom of Information Act (FOIA) request and ask (with a recorder on) "Under what grounds am I being denied access?" and name the record and person refusing on the recording, in case you need to file a formal complaint. (See Search Tip #20 in this chapter, "Freedom of Information Act and the Privacy Act.")

31. CORRECTING A RECORD. If a record has significant errors (other than harmless typos), you are entitled to have the record corrected. Whether by brief letter identifying the record and error, or by court order depends on the record. During litigation, a record related to the litigation and in need of correction would need to be presented or argued at a hearing since the judge may need to decide its accuracy (for instance if it's in regard to testimony or evidence) according to judge's discretion. After a case is closed, generally the record cannot be changed except by creating a subsequent record on appeal.

32. PRISONER LOCATOR WEBSITES. If the person you seek has or may have a criminal record and is presently incarcerated, the Department of Corrections (DOC) for the state you are searching may have a free Prisoner Locator link on their website, as that will tell if the prison the person is presently incarcerated in that state and at which prison, and you can then bring up the address designated for prisoner mail at that prison. For some states, however, you may need to request the location of an inmate by phoning or writing to the State Department of Corrections. Some DOC websites also identify the county jail where the person may be held or indicate that the person is currently released on probation. If so, the probation office for the locale can tell you the name and contact information for the person's probation officer who, in turn, may be able to tell you where to contact the person or may agree to pass a message to the person when they comply with periodically reporting to the probation office.

There are also privately owned websites that offer criminal background checks and prisoner locator services for a fee but if a state does not provide prisoner locating, then chances are slim that any other service can do so, even if they have arrest records indicating disposition of criminal cases.

There are also Sex Offender mandatory registration registries online, by neighborhood.

Genealogy databases may include prison records, old prison records in other countries, U.S. Civil War Prison search engines, and Prisoner of War records (see Search Tip #36 for Military and Prisoner of War records)

33. DNA TESTING RECORDS. DNA tests have long been used to prove paternity and family relationships for inheritance, etc. When adoptees or donor offspring and their biological parents wish proof of their biological relationship, affordable DNA testing and matching to find the same DNA profile, if available from a number of sources in their database. They include:
•DNA Tests ($99 Autosomal) - http://23andMe.com
•Family Tree DNA ($60 Autosomal) - http://FamilyTreeDNA.com
•Ancestry.com ($99 Autosomal and Y-Chromosome)- http://Ancestry.com
•Home DNA Testing - http://www.homedna.com/paternity
•DNA Testing by Mail - http://www.gtldna.com/RelationshipTesting/
•Upload DNA Test Results (just from 23andMe) - http://GedMatch.com

You can also create a page on Facebook with your DNA results for matching to possible siblings, others. Criminal arrest and proceedings may involve biological evidence such as blood, saliva or semen, or the articles on which DNA can be found. If DNA testing may prove exculpatory to an innocent to a wrongfully convicted Defendant but the Defendant was refused a DNA test, or a DNA test was done before conviction prior to new science, most states have a Penal Code section based on the Federal Innocence Protection Act that entitles a wrongfully convicted person to Post-Conviction DNA testing by a designated lab, upon court approval.

34. VOTER REGISTRATION. Voter registrations are public records in County Clerks' offices. You can write for them but it will take forever to hear back. Especially in cities understaffed or cutting services to the public to save costs. In many area, these records are available online. If not, a trip to the County Clerk's office may be your best bet.

35. FEDERAL RESOURCES include "The Federal Parent Locator," used to access Internal Revenue Service (IRS) tax records (IRS records are not "public" records, though tax accountants routinely and legally tap into certain IRS databases); Social Security records (previously detailed in this chapter); military locator services (see Search Tip #36 for all branches of military); National Archives Office of Disclosure, and Immigration and Naturalization Services (INS) records.

      NCIC - THE NATIONAL CRIMINAL IDENTIFICATION CENTER database is not accessible by the public. DO NOT TRY TO OBTAIN INFORMATION FROM A FEDERAL EMPLOYEE THAT IS NOT OBTAINABLE WITH A SIMPLE WRITTEN REQUEST CITING THE FREEDOM OF INFORMATION ACT (See Search Tip #39 for more on FOIA requests).

36. THE NATIONAL CENSUS can be used to conduct a search by age. Although censuses are a source of genealogical information, the Census Bureau does not provide these data. The Census Bureau is not able to locate missing persons, or provide recent information on individuals. The Census Bureau provides an "age search" service to the public by searching confidential records from the Federal population censuses of 1910 to 2010 and will issue an official transcript of the results for a congressionally mandated fee - Census Bureau Home page is at https://www.census.gov/#

      NOTE: Information can be released only to the named person, his/her heirs, or legal representatives. Individuals can use these transcripts, which may contain information on a person's age, sex, race, State or country of birth, and relationship to the householder, as evidence to qualify for Social Security and other retirement benefits, in making passport applications, to prove relationship in settling estates, in genealogy research, etc., or to satisfy other situations where a birth or other certificate may be needed but is not available. For questions regarding the age search service, please contact the National Processing Center at (812) 218-3046. Their fax number is (812) 218-3371. There is a fee required (quoted in 2014 as $65, but ask) for a search of one Census for one person only. Personal checks and money orders accepted. No credit cards. Years Searched: 1910 through 2010. Census records with individual names are not on computer. They are on microfilm, arranged according to the address at the time of the census. Most agencies require the earliest Census after the date of birth. A completed BC-600 Application form [PDF - 142k] is required for Search of Census Records, signed by the person for whom the search is to be conducted. This person may authorize the results to be sent to another person/agency by also completing Item 3 of the Application.

      Information regarding a child who has not yet reached the legal age of 18 may be obtained by written request of either parent or guardian. A guardian must provide a copy of the court order naming them as such. Information regarding mentally incompetent persons may be obtained upon the written request of the legal representative, supported by a copy of the court order naming such legal representation. With egard to deceased persons, the Application must be signed by (1) a blood relative in the immediate family (parent, child, brother, sister, grandparent), (2) the surviving wife or husband, (3) the administrator or executor of the estate, or (4) a beneficiary by will or insurance. In all cases involving deceased persons, a copy of the death certificate MUST be provided and the relationship to the deceased MUST be stated on the application. Legal representatives MUST also furnish a copy of the court order naming such legal representatives, and beneficiaries MUST furnish legal evidence of such beneficiary evidence. An official Census transcript will list the person's name, relationship to household head, age at the time of the census, and state of birth. Citizenship will be provided if the person was foreign born. Single items of data (such as occupation for Black Lung cases) can be provided upon request.

If a person is not found, a form will be sent with that information. Additional data on the same person, called the Full Schedule, is the complete one line entry of personal data recorded for that individual ONLY. This will be furnished in addition to the regular transcript. The additional charge (quoted in 2014 as $10, but ask) for each full schedule. They are not available for 1970, 1980, 1990 and 2000. State of birth and citizenship is only available in census records from 1910 to 1950. The normal processing time is 3 to 4 weeks. Cases are processed on a first in, first out basis. Passport and other priority cases can be processed in a week or less. To expedite, there is an additional fee required. To receive results within three days, the application will need to be sent by Next-Day Air via the Post Office, Federal Express, or private carrier and enclose a pre-paid express return envelope. Applications can be faxed to you.

37. PHONE RECORDS, UNLISTED PHONE NUMBERS, ADDRESSES. Public Directory listings by Name and City/State at http://WhilePages.com may include the person's listed phone number and sometimes an otherwise unlisted/unpublished phone number as result of the person having divulged their phone number on an unsecured website, or to a company that shares or sells mailing lists with such information to advertisers. "People Search" and "Intellius" are two sites that will sell same-name listings that include phone numbers without guarantee that they are current. Public libraries maintain databases compiled from nationwide mailing lists which are sold and re-sold (hence those annoying unsolicited sales calls, even to your unlisted number). Cell phone companies are one source of such lists as subscribers often forget or are unaware that they must opt out or specify that their phone number is not to be listed or published.

Directory Assistance Operators may share an address, especially if you state that you need to be sure you have the right party at the right address before dialing the number to avoid being charged for a wrong number. If the operator refuses, or will only share the street name but not the house number, simply dial back--you'll get a different operator who may be more willing or able.

Licensed private investigators, like Law Enforcement, may be able to obtain phone records and non-published phone numbers from telephone service representatives, using only name and zip code. The general public may be told that telephone operators and service representatives do not have access to these numbers, but if, for instance, you owe money, you can bet a collections agency will have your phone number in an instant.

Amateur searchers can possibly elicit such information using ruses, but if they make a false representation especially in a phone call that crosses state lines, be aware that is then a federal crime that has resulted in arrest by the FBI and imprisonment of not only the searcher impersonating an official to get information across state lines, but also the person who headed the organization in which the searcher was employed with headquarters in yet a different state. (See Disclaimer at the front of this book, and more about harmless ruses versus prosecutable offenses in the final chapter: "STARTING YOUR OWN SEARCH BUSINESS."

38. OCCUPATIONAL, RECREATIONAL LICENSES and REGISTRATIONS.

LABOR UNIONS will not cooperate with Law Enforcement but private searchers have been successful in eliciting information for locating people via their Labor Unions by claiming they need to get in touch with the person due to a family emergency. CAUTION: If someone offers to leave a message instead, avoid doing so, since you will then be sharing your phone number without knowing theirs and you don't want to start off on the wrong foot by having to explain that you made up a story to get their phone number. So, instead, explain to the person at the Labor union that it's a delicate matter that may upset the other person to hear it from a stranger and is best told by a supportive relative/personal friend but you've lost the number. If this goes against your personal ethics, then simply ask to "verify the phone number which may have been changed." This implies you had the number to begin with, and any number you suggest will be wrong and hopefully the person will provide the correct one. Some agencies may also provide proof of an Occupational License but with identifying information blackened out. Such a record may still be helpful to verify an occupation, etc.

HUNTING AND FISHING LICENSES are public records which disclose last reported address etc.

39. FREEDOM OF INFORMATION ACT and THE PRIVACY ACT: You can obtain a copy of The Federal Freedom of Information Act (FOIA), and THE PRIVACY ACT online (see http://www.foia.gov/ and http://en.wikipedia.org/wiki/Privacy_Act_of_1974), or from your public library, or from your local Congressman's office without charge. Although the two laws were enacted for different purposes, and pertain only to records held by FEDERAL agencies in a "system of records" retrieved by name or personal identifier, there is some similarity in their provisions. There may be a difference in fees, time limits and exemptions from access.

STATE FOIA LAWS in every state pertain only to state-held records. The FOIA laws by state, are available online at the State Freedom of Information Coalition (NFOIC) website at http://www.nfoic.org/state-freedom-of-information-laws by clicking on the abbreviation for the name of the state. Some state FOIA laws contain multiple exemptions of records that cannot be accessed, even under the State FOIA.

The FEDERAL FOIA gives "any person" the right to access, while THE PRIVACY ACT gives only the person named in the record the right of access.

Sample letters for obtaining records using the FOIA can be found online also.

If you request records about YOURSELF under both Federal and State FOIA laws, federal agencies may withhold records from ONLY to the extent that they are exempt under BOTH federal and state FOIA. FOIA requests require fees. But if you want any information about yourself without fees, just cite The Privacy Act. If in doubt as to which law will satisfy your needs, cite both. In any case, you need to "reasonably describe" the specific record(s) you seek to avoid delay from not sufficiently describing the record.

To obtain records about OTHER PEOPLE, the FOIA contains a very important provision concerning personal privacy: "Exemption 6" protects you from others who may seek information about you and it may also block you if you seek information about others. Exemption 6 also permits an agency to withhold information about individuals if disclosing it would be "clearly unwarranted invasion of personal privacy," but Exemption 6 cannot be used by an agency to withhold information about yourself. Therefore, searchers sometimes request information in the name of the person the information is about. To be covered by Exemption 6, (1) The information requested must be about an "identifiable" individual; (2) an invasion of that individual's personal privacy if disclosed to others; (3) clearly unwarranted" to disclose.

ADOPTEES AND THE FOIA. Yet the FOIA exempts adoptees' own birth records by vaguely wording the law while at the same time the law recognizes the adoptee's basic human right to know his own identity and origins. No one has yet successfully challenged adoption secrecy laws under the FOIA and Privacy Act because the United States Supreme Court simply refuses to hear such cases (as tried by ALMA Society v. Mellon, and Yesterday's Children v Kennedy in the 1970s. What made Carangelo v. Wiecker in 1990 "different" was that the U.S. Supreme Court deferred to the state legislatures, despite that it presented an important federal question and challenge to the federal Constitutionality of "government protected child stealing under color of state adoption secrecy laws."

40. HIRING A LICENSE PRIVATE INVESTIGATOR {PI). While this book enables you to conduct your own search, if you should be considering hiring a licensed Private Investigator to conduct a search for you, ask the PI for his/her resume, references, license number and whether he/she is bonded. If you need a search for an adoptee or parent of an adoptee, a PI may not be experienced or willing to do such a search. The best detectives have ample experience and the best indicator of that is word of mouth as reputations are hard won in this business. A bond larger than the minimum may be available for a broad investigation that could cover several states or even a foreign country. Interview him or her for at least 20 minutes to discuss your needs and how they would be met. Check the state licensing division to be sure the PI's record is clean, and require a signed agreement defining fees and the specific service(s) to be provided within a time frame, with periodic reporting if likely to take a considerable amount of time, or stating that you require that the PI document what they did and observed for a court case.

Times have changed for PIs. Instead of snapping incriminating photos to support claims in divorce cases, most modern "private eyes" earn bigger fees from corporate spying, security and personnel matters. They are often more effective than police in tracking down runaway or missing children because they can focus on leads for a single client, whereas a Missing Persons Bureau may have 30 cases at a time. If a PI can't produce a hard lead within 3 days, s/he may be incompetent or stalling to run up the bill.

41. ADOPTION SEARCHERS. (See also "Chapter 2: "With or Without a Name.) Amateur searchers, as well as agencies who charge flat search fees may or may not have a "No find, no fee" policy and it doesn't hurt to ask for such terms. Try to determine whether they have "tools of the trade" such as innovative technical devices and computer programs or databases, and /or a network of human resources to tap. Most licensed private investigators do not have resources nor motivation for adoption searches so may cite "sealed records" as preventing their access to information or ear of jeopardizing their license by venturing into adoptee/parent searches. In a recent TNT Network TV series, "APB with Troy Dunn," Troy "The Locator" Dunn unites separated loved ones using new technology and a phone app to solve the case within the minutes between TV commercials. It's good that the general public be shown the damage done by needless family separations, the need for family reunifications and how to respect the sensitivities of the involved parties via such dramatizations; however behind the scenes in the real world, solving "impossible searches" usually requires tipsters

and cash that someone has to afford, or a dedicated "Search Angel" who most often is an adoptee, or a mother who lost a child to adoption, and who now works tediously without compensation to help other adoptees and parents of closed adoptions connect by discovering bits and pieces of information that, in time, result in solving the adoption puzzle. (See also 'RESOURCES and WEBSITES" section)

In the 1980s, before computers were commonplace in every office and household, and through the 1990s, AMERICANS FOR OPEN RECORDS (AmFOR.net) reunited 20,000 families by developing a network of individuals throughout the United States, Canada, the United Kingdom and Australia, and also learned techniques applicable in other countries, to assist adoptees and parents in overcoming the roadblocks that separated them. And it was all done by mail and phone. We often published their stories and provided media with their "live" reunions to acquaint the general public with the idea that "nothing bad" happens when adoptions are opened up. Even though a handful of states have enacted legislation permitting adult adoptees to obtain their original, unfalsified birth certificates, and even though so-called "open" adoptions have increased, the records are still closed to the adoptee's and parents' access, so each new generation is searching for people and answers.

42. SEARCH WORLDWIDE. The worldwide search network consists of thousands of professional, semi-professional and lay-researchers including adoption searchers (most of whom are, themselves, adoptees and parents) and also genealogists. Some searchers will work only on a one-to-one basis while others work only through group membership and support.

Local search and support groups and individuals tend to specialize in their local area. National search and support groups usually require a membership fee and may hold meetings. Individuals and groups that offer search assistance may also belong to an umbrella organization such as Concerned United Birthparents (http:/cubirthparents.org/), the American Adoption Congress (http://americanadoptioncongress.org/), Bastard Nation (http://bastards.org/), Americans For Open Records (http://AmFOR.net), for a unified presence in media, and for lobbying, fund raising, book sales, and/or annual national conference lectures, workshops, demonstrations. AmFOR continues to produce updated versions of two essential "how to" search books, *The Ultimate Search Book- Worldwide Edition*, which contains both "how to" information and resources for every state and 200 countries, currently published by Clearfield Books, and *The Ultimate Search Book-- U.S. Edition*" in e-book format published by Access Press - both are available from Amazon.com and Barnes and Noble at BN.com.

43. REAL ESTATE LISTINGS. Type a street address with city and state in the search field at Zillow.com and it will bring up the real estate listing for the home whether or not it is currently for sale and provide information about the type and age of the home, the area it's in, when it originally and last sold and for what price, its suggested current value, exterior and interior photos, etc. Just type the street and number, city and state in the Google search field. Google's 360-degree aerial views and street views can be manipulated to enable a virtual drive through the neighborhood and beyond.

44. MILITARY PERSONNEL AND RECORDS. The Department of Veterans Affairs has a Nationwide Grave Locator http://gravelocator.cem.va.gov/for locating deceased military personnel.

Or, to find active, former/retired, or deceased military personnel or records, each branch of the military has its own department(s) to assist according to the status of the person (see below for address and phone number – Check online in case of change of address or phone.). When writing to any branch of service, your request should include at least the following information, or, if many of he items are unknown, at least the first 5 items: (1) Full name under which the service was performed; (2) Social Security Number; (3) Dates of Service; (4) Date and Place of Birth; (5) Residence of service member at time of entry into the service; (6) Branch of service; (7) Reserve status, Branch and dates; (8) Last known address; (9) Grade or Rank; (10) Name and Address of Service Person's Parents; (11) Organizations with approximate Dates Assigned (the most significant ones).

But when little information is known, one technique for preventing return of the inquiry for "insufficient information" (whether online or by mail) is to approximate or make up some of the unknown information and see what comes back, perhaps auto-corrected. A service person may obtain all the information in his/her own record. The person's next-of-kin, if the veteran is deceased, and federal offices, for official purposes, are authorized to receive certain types of information. Other requesters need permission of the service person. Fees are determined at the time the records are released, but you should always inquire as to how fees are calculated – for instance, a per-page copy fee with minimum fee for under "x" number of pages.

If you are adopted but know the name of one or both of your biological parent(s) and that they were military personnel at one time, in order to be considered "next of kin" for purpose of obtaining information or records. Omit any mention of being adopted.

AIR FORCE. For all reserve members not on extended duty and all retired reservists in a non-pay status: Air Reserve Personnel Center, 3800 York Street, Denver, CO 80205-9998. For all Active Duty personnel, all personnel on a temporary disability retired list (TDRL), general officers in a retired (pay) status: USAF Military Personnel Center, Military Personnel Records Div., Randolph AFB, TX 78148-9997; (210) 656-2660 (will only confirm in writing).

ARMY. Officers separated before July 1, 1917, enlisted personnel separated before November 1, 1912: National Archives and Records Service, National Archives Bldg,Washington, DC 20408-0001. All retired personnel, all Reserve personnel (includes retired Reservists): Commander, U.S. Army Reserve Personnel Center, 9700 Page Blvd., St. Louis, MO 63132-5200. All officers on active duty: Commander, U.S. Army Military Personnel Center, Management and Support Div, Officer Records Branch, 200 Stovall St, Alexandria, VA 22332-0400. Enlisted personnel on active duty: Commander, U.S. Army Enlisted Records and Evaluation Center, Fort Benjamin Harrison, IN 46240-5301; (703) 325-3732 (will only confirm in writing).

ARMY NATIONAL GUARD. All members not on active duty in the U.S. Army, personnel discharged from the National Guard (excludes records of periods and active duty for training in the U.S. Army): The Adjutant General (of the appropriate state, DC, or Commonwealth of Puerto Rico). Records for periods of active duty or active duty for training for the U.S. Army for periods ending after December 31,1959: Headquarters, Department of the Army, Office of the Adjutant General, U.S. Army Reserve Components Personnel and Administration Center, 9700 Page Blvd., St. Louis, MO 63132-5200.

COAST GUARD: Enlisted personnel separated less than 6 months, Officer personnel separated less than 3 months, all active Coast Guard members of the Reserves, Officer personnel separated before January 1, 1929: Commandant, U.S. Coast Guard, U.S. Coast Guard, Washington, DC 20221-0001; (203) 227-2229 (will confirm some by phone).

MARINE CORPS. Officer personnel on active duty or in Reserves, enlisted personnel on active duty or in organized active Reserves, all personnel completely separated less than 4 months: Commandant of the Marine Corps, Headquarters, U.S. Marine Corps, Washington, DC 20380-0001; (703) 784-3942 (will confirm by phone).

NAVY. Officers on active duty, those separated less than one year, all Officers with rank of Admiral, enlisted personnel on active duty and those separated with less than 4 months, active and inactive Reservists with 18 or more months remaining in first term of enlistment: Chief of Naval Personnel, Department of the Navy, Washington, DC 20360-00011 (901) 874-3388+ press 2 (will confirm by phone).

ALL BRANCHES. If your request does not pertain to any of the above categories, address an inquiry to: ATT: (appropriate branch of service) Records, 9700 Page Blvd., St. Louis, MO 63132

VETERANS REUNIONS INFORMATION: VETS, PO Box 901, Columbia, MO 65205; (573) 474-4444. Also" REUNIONS, VFW Magazine, 406 W. 34th Street, Ste. 523, Kansas City, MO 64111.

WWII VET FATHERS information is available as result of WAR BABES 1988 lawsuit. Contact the Dept. of Defense, Pentagon, Washington, DC (They will not provide the street address.

CIVIL WAR SOLDIERS and SAILORS. To locate either a Union or Confederate Civil War Soldier or Sailor by name, there is an online database. "Soldiers and Sailors Database" at http://www.nps.gov/civilwar/index.htm - sponsored by the National Parks Service, a free service – most other websites for finding Civil War soldiers may offer free registration but then charge for access to their databases and/or records. For descendants of Confederate Soldiers, the following provides links, by state, to resources - http://jrw3.tripod.com/do.htm

MILITARY, WAR and LINEAGE SOCIETIES - CYNDI'S LIST has several pages of Links to these websites - http://cyndislist.com/societies/lineage/military/

45. PASSPORT SERVICES AS AN INFORMATION SOURCE. For adoptees denied their original birth certificates, applying for a passport can generate a request for their original birth certificate. The amended version issued to adoptees may be considered a "delayed" or withheld as fraudulent if the date of issue is months or years later than the date of birth, depending on date of adoption. Passport Services needs the original to verify citizenship. Request the court provide YOU with an Order ordering Vital Records to release your original birth certificate to YOU for purpose of obtaining a passport; attach proof of your application for a passport and response from Passport Services. This has worked for some when the clerks release the birth certificate to the adoptee instead of to Passport Services. If your immigrant ancestors returned home to visit family or to bring relatives to America, they may have had a U.S. Passport. For passports prior to 1906, write to: Diplomatic Records Branch of the National Archives, Washington, DC 20406. For Passport applications after 1906, write to: Passport Office, U.S. Department of States, 1425 "K: Street, Washington, DC 20406.

46. MEDIA ACCESS TO INFORMATION AND RECORDS. A good local source of non-legal advice for accessing information and obtaining records is your local newspaper and TV station's investigative reporter or assignment editor, since they need to know the law and how to legally obtain information, with or without a court order. If you have a good news story or human interest story to share, they may be willing to advise you on their approach to obtaining information or records to back up a story, such as sources that may provide information that a sealed record contains. A reporter won't reveal his whistle blower sources but may be able to point you to files that you can access

47. MEDIA SUPPORTED SEARCHES. Local media attention to a search for a missing person can garner community support with people joining the search. National media attention to an adoption mystery can produce leads or even solve the case. In #48, below, I was denied Good Cause action by a court but publicity drew the attention of a searcher who quickly found my son for a price.

48. GOOD CAUSE. In any state, regardless of any provisions for disclosure, an adoptee has the right to request that the court open his/her adoption file "for Good Cause." Because the law does not specifically address what constitutes "Good Cause," the matter is entirely at the discretion of judges, who usually deny the request, often citing "privacy" of the "birth" mother, despite that sealing of records was never requested, but was imposed by law. (If you know your "birth" mother is deceased, see "Adoption Search Tips # 9" in the next chapter.) In the 1980s. this author requested Judge Glen Knierim of Connecticut's Probate Court to open her son's adoption file "for Good Cause" as Connecticut law allowed adoptees but not the adoptees' biological parents, in this case to communicate important new medical information about an inheritable heart defect. The Judge was quoted by a journalist as saying the reason he denied the request was *"because the law doesn't compel me to do so."* This is why anyone contemplating the "Good Cause" option should consult and be represented by an attorney.

49. 'WORD OF MOUTH." People can be excellent sources of information when the information they are willing to share can be verified. It's important to regard verbal information as a "lead," rather than an absolute fact. Neighbors can be a good source of information depending on your approach, for instance, if you're thinking of buying a home and was wondering whether it is a quiet street, whether the residents are in your age group, etc. An adoptee's unknown parent's name, spelled out by a sympathetic social worker at risk of her job in a medically urgent situation, is probably reliable but still requires verification and followup to locate. Consider the source and verify!

50. ONE SEARCH ENDS, ANOTHER MAY BEGIN. While most searches may end when the person sought is located, after an adoptee who finds their biological mother, the next question usually asked is "Who is my father?" (See Adoption Search Tip#10, "Finding Dad," in the next chapter.)

STATES THAT PERMIT VARYING DEGREES OF RECORDS ACCESS, 2014

- **12 states, as of June 2014, allow adult Adoptees "unrestricted access"** to their own original birth **certificates (by simply presenting their ID):**
  AL, AK, DE, KS, NE (age 25), NH, NJ, OH (pre-1964), PA, OR, VA, WI (w/Parent's consent)

- **2 states allow unrestricted access depending on year of birth:**
  ME (pre-6/1947), MT (pre-1967), IA (pre-1947)

- **5 states allow access to Adoptee, subject to "veto" by the biological parent:**
  CO, CT, NE, TN, RI

- **3 states and DC have NO provisions whatsoever for obtaining information post-adoption, except by court order for "good cause,"** [impossible to obtain]:
  NC, VT, WY, DC

- **ALL states except DC provide non-identifying information to** *adult Adoptees*

- **ALL states provide non-identifying information to A***dopters*

- **21 states** provide **non-identifying information to** *"Birth" Parents:*
  AL, AZ, AR, CA, CT, DE, HI, IN, MD, MA, MI, MN, NM, NC, OK, OR, RI, SC, UT, VT, WA.

Chapter 2:
WITH OR WITHOUT A NAME
Families Separated by Adoption or Divorce

- privacy - (the state of not being seen by others by one's own choice)
- confidentiality - (imposed in a discretionary manner, avoiding accountability)
- secrecy - (imposed concealment, enabling coverup, avoiding accountability)

Americans For Open Records (AmFOR) has, for years, successfully completed "No Name Searches" which are searches without a known name to start, usually due to closed adoption, or due to divorce that may entail a stepparent adoption by the custodial parent where the absent parent may have changed their name from re-marriage. This chapter reveals techniques that adoptees and parents can utilize for obtaining the unknown name, and for adoptees and children of divorce searching for biological family members, and for parents searching for their children.

STEP 1 - WHICH STATE? There are usually two adoption files – one held by the public Social Services, or private adoption agency or attorney, and one filed in the court since adoptions must be finalized by a court. An adoptee, or a parent who has voluntarily relinquished or otherwise lost a child to adoption, first needs to know in what state the adoption was finalized, which is often the adopter's state of residence, so the court of jurisdiction may be the court may also be in the county where the adopter resides. But also, a child may have been adopted out of state via an attorney or private nonprofit adoption agency. If you don't know, and Social Services finds no record, it may be that it was a private adoption. In the past, many agencies had failed to try to collect sufficient information on a child's biological family and pre-adoption past, or provided as little summarized information as possible, even untrue information, while others provided a great deal of factual information if available, and even actual records, though they may have been "blocked" (names blackened out). As the times, politics, laws and attitudes changed, so did their methods and extent of collection and disclosure of adoption information by some agencies.

STEP 2 - WHAT'S THE LAW?
When you know which state finalized the adoption, you can find out what the current state law is "for post-adoption disclosure" in that state (which could be a different state from the state in which the adoptee was born). State laws now mandate provision of at least "non-identifying" background information to the adult adoptee.

Some include the parent or adopter. On the previous page, you will find a chart listing the states, alphabetically, and indicating whether, to whom, and how disclosure can be provided in each state, including by means of: adoptee access to Original Birth Certificate at legal age; a state reunion registry and who may register; identifying information or contact by mutual consent; and a Court Appointed Confidential Intermediary to locate and contact the other party.

NON-IDENTIFYING INFORMATION. All states now mandate by law the provision of "Non-Identifying" information to an adult adoptee. Not all provide Non-Identifying information to biological parents or adopters. Approximately 15 states allow biological adult siblings of the adoptee to seek and access Non-Identifying information.

Non-identifying information can provide useful clues for discovering identities and locating the other person, depending on what information was collected at the time of the adoption, but also may inform the adoptee of his/her family's previously unknown nationality, parents' ages at time of the birth and/or adoption, the adoptee's age when adopted, the parents' race, religion, education level, employment, pre-existing siblings, circumstances, etc. Parents can discover the adopters' ages at time of the adoption, nationality, race, religion, education level, employment, pre-existing children by birth or adoption, etc. Every state now mandates, by law, that public and private adoption agencies and attorneys must provide adult adoptees and their biological parents with each other's non-identifying background information upon written request, usually with proof of identity and age such as a driver's license. If you're the adoptee, your letter should list at the top your adoptive parents' full names (since your adoption file is filed by their names); your date and place of birth, the date and state your adoption was finalized, if known; and any other known related names, dates, places, and your Waiver of Confidentiality. Ask ALL of the questions on the list below, even if you believe you already know some of the answers.

If you're the parent who lost a child to adoption, your letter should begin with your child's date and place of birth, agency or attorney that facilitated the adoption and in what county and state, your full name at time of the relinquishment, any other known related names, dates, places,

your current contact information and Waiver of Confidentiality. Ask ALL of the questions listed below, even if you believe you already know some of the answers.

WAIVER OF CONFIDENTIALITY. If both the adoptee and parent have provided their "Waiver of Confidentiality" to the adoption agency, attorney and/or court, identifying information and contact may be facilitated in states that permit it post-adoption. Such a Waiver may not need to be on a specific form for the purpose. There may be a letter from the adoptee or parent, placed in the adoption file, stating that the adoptee or parent waives their confidentiality in the event the other party seeks information or contact in the future. It may or may not require notarization but it's always a good idea to do so. If, when your Waiver form or letter is placed in the adoption file, the other party's Waiver is already in the file, you may be informed of any further steps required to enable contact with the other party, depending on state law and agency policy and procedure.

POST-ADOPTION REUNION REGISTRIES. Due to a proliferation of private online and offline adoptee-parent reunion registries, including over 400 listed by Adoption.com at http://reunion-registries.adoption.com/, most adoption search and support organizations now advise their members to register primarily on the (free) private nonprofit INTERNATIONAL SOUNDEX REUNION REGISTRY (See Tip #7 for details) to take the control away from agencies. But it cannot be searched online, so you must remember to update your contact information if you have a change of address or phone because ISRR will need this to inform both parties if there is a "match." Large, free, online registries include Cyndi's List at CyndisList.com and The Seeker at http://www.the-seeker.com/

A California registry, "Find My Family Registry" http://www.findmyfamily.org/California, has over 11,000 registrants and can be searched online.

In states that offer a State Adoption Reunion Registry via the agency that facilitated the adoption, it is more often a matter of providing such a Waiver to the file, so may not have instantaneous results, although some agencies now have on online registry . In past years, there was a proliferation of private adoptee-parent-sibling reunion registries which provide registration online or by mail. Online registries can be searched by either party. Some are totally free while others require a one-time or annual membership fee, and an abundance of registries may lessen the chance of a random "match" if the other party is not clairvoyant to know on which the first party may have, by chance, registered.

BIRTH ANNOUNCEMENTS in newspaper archives may automatically been published in a newspaper if a notation stating "Do Not Publish" by hospital staff was not evident at the time to advise that the newborn is to be adopted. When searching for a birth notice, request a range of up to 4 weeks AFTER date of birth. Whether the newspaper maintains archives online, or whether you can order copies of actual new clips direct from the newspaper office's "morgue" or "library" for a copy fee, or from public libraries, they may reveal the parents' names to a searching adoptee.

MARRIAGE RECORDS, DIVORCE RECORDS, VOTER REGISTRATIONS, PROPERTY OWNERSHIP AND TAX RECORDS. In states where marriage and divorce records are public records, a vital records office may be able to cross reference a mother's known maiden or married name at time of the adoptee's birth with any subsequent name change via divorce and later marriage records. When you have a name, voter registrations, property ownership and tax assessments at Tax Assessor's office are always public records. There is also usually a Real Estate Index at the County Courthouse, a courthouse Litigation Index, court dockets (of even adoption hearings and dockets are public records, not sealed) while there is restricted access to the court Petition to Adopt and Final Decree of Adoption.

Other publicly accessible records include Church Baptismal Records (see Search Tip #5); Mormon Family History Center Library records of births and genealogies worldwide; White Pages directories, especially http://WhitePages.com; Yellow Pages and other business directories; Criss-Cross directories, and High School Yearbooks (see Search Tip# 3).

QUESTIONS FOR ADOPTEES TO ASK AGENCY AND COURT:

1. What was the reason for my relinquishment?

2. What were the ages of my parents?

3. Where were my parents born, and where did they reside at the time of my adoption? Were they from same area where I was born?

4. Name of hospital where I was born?

5. What are the nationalities of my parents?

6. Were my grandparents living?

7. Educational background of my parents and grandparents?

8. Occupations and social history of parents and grandparents?

9. Any siblings?

10. Were parents married? Divorced? Previous marriages?

11. Religion of parents?

12. Was I in a foster home? How long? Who were my foster parents?

13. How long between relinquishment & placement?

14. Was my mother in a maternity home? Did she see & hold me? Was she counseled before/after delivery or signing?

15. Color of parents' hair? Eyes? Their height? Weight?

16. Did my parents have brothers, sisters? Ages?

17. Mother's first name and initial?

18. Did she name me? What name?

19. Were my parents active in school activities? What kind?

20. How much did I weigh at birth?

21. Has my mother or any birth family member EVER contacted the agency? Any letters, photos or mementos in my adoption file? Is there any Waiver of Confidentiality in my adoption file?

22. Name of social worker handling my placement?

23. Date adoption was finalized? What court(s) initiating, finalizing?

24. Please provide me a copy of the court proceedings and final decree.

25. Please provide me with all medical information on my birth family.

26. Please place my Waiver of Confidentiality in the agency file.

27. Please contact my parents and inform them my updated Waiver of Confidentiality has been provided to the file.

QUESTIONS FOR PARENTS TO ASK AGENCY AND COURT:

1. Regarding the adopter(s):

   a. what were their ages?

   b. where were they born?

   c. what are their nationalities? religion?

   d. any siblings of adoptive parents?

   e. length of marriage at time of adoption?

   f. any previous marriages or divorces?

   g. other children by birth or adoption?

   h. deaths in family?

   i. medical histories, diseases?

   j. did they own their own home?

   k. professions, occupations, education?

   l. where residing at time of adoption?

   m. where do they now reside?

   n. reason given for adopting?

2. Regarding the child, please provide physical description when last seen by agency, court or attorney.

3. Was child in foster care? How long? Names of foster parents?

4. Date adoption was finalized? What court?

5. Please provide a copy of the relinquishment I signed and the original birth certificate issued to me.

6. What is the name of the social worker who handled the placement?

7. Has adoptee or adopter(s) contacted agency since adoption?

8. What was and is my child's physical and emotional health?

9. Were the adoptive parents advised to tell child of adoption?

10. What information on me was given to adoptive parents?

11. Please place my Waiver of Confidentiality in the file.

12. What agency/court/attorney will transmit my request for contact to the adoptee or adopter(s)?

Adoptees and their biological families confront an adversarial adoption system designed to thwart their efforts to locate each other. It has been reported by some that even when both parties have registered on state-sponsored mutual consent voluntary registries, state agencies fail to "match" and inform the parties that each has registered and have consented to be contacted. The state usually does not publicize their registries or law and policy changes nor solicit a missing Waiver of Confidentiality in behalf of the other party who has submitted their Waiver and desires information and/or contact. And when they do inquire, they may have to pay hefty fees and wait months for a response. Los Angeles County Social Services, for example, often took a year to respond. When individuals complete searches on their own, some discover that each was registered with the state for a year or more, or that each had informed the agency and/or court of urgency for medical or other reasons, or that the other party has died.

Still, state registries should not be overlooked as reunions have resulted for those who cannot or do not wish to actively search, or who wish to utilize every means available.

ADOPTION SEARCH TIPS (which may also apply to stepparent adoptions):

1. READ CHAPTER 1: SEARCH BASICS.

2. DETERMINE THE STATE in which your adoption was finalized because the court in that state, and possibly an agency, holds your adoption file(s).

3. DETERMINE LAW in that state on disclosure of adoption information and access to records, particularly access to your original birth certificate (See Chart but also ask in case the law changes).

4. LOCATE YOUR ADOPTION FILE(S). Your best bet is to ask your adopters which agency and court facilitated your adoption if you don't already know and if your adopters do not have records to provide you. If you cannot obtain this information from your adopters, the central office of Social Services at the state's capital city, can tell you if it was a public Social Services agency and which branch. If no record, chances are it was a private agency or attorney which they would not have record of. Since the agency and Court that finalized the adoption is usually in the county where the adopter resided at the time of placement, it would not be too hard to find the Court and agency that has your adoption files by looking up the Court and all adoption agencies in that county, and if no luck then look up adoption attorneys in that county.

5. REQUEST YOUR NON-IDENTIFYING INFORMATION from both the Court of jurisdiction and the agency that holds your adoption file, by asking ALL of the Questions listed in this chapter.

6. PROVIDE YOUR WAIVER OF CONFIDENTIALITY and your request for identifying information to both the agency and court at the same time you request your Non-Identifying Information. Request the Petition To Adopt and Final Decree of Adoption from the Court.

7. BROWSE THE COURT DOCKETS for the dates you were relinquished for adoption and also when the adoption was finalized (generally automatically, without necessity for hearing, one year from date of Relinquishment of Parental Rights and placement in your adoptive home, but there will still be a docket notation). Court dockets are publicly viewable records in Probate, Circuit, and Family Courts or similar named courts; not sealed; and even though your biological parents are most likely not in court, their names may appear on the earlier docket while your adopter's name appears on the latter docket. Fortunately they can be cross-referenced by same Case Number, so that if you find the Final Decree case number by the date, you can check one year prior for the Relinquishment and Petition to Adopt using the same Case Number.

8. REQUEST THE PETITION and FINAL DECREE OF ADOPTION. Years ago, Court Clerks were instructed to "block" names on these documents with an indelible black ink marker before providing the document to the adult adoptee. Unless the blackened information has also been photocopied after blackened, first try photocopying the BACK side of the document on a very dark setting to see if typewritten impressions appear. Or, the impressions left by older typewriters can be revealed by penciling the back of the document where the names would be and thereby revealing the names (just backwards). Try removing the black marker ink with a dab of hairspray or cologne (alcohol based) on a q-tip. Since this will wet and possibly smudge it's tried last.

9. DECEASED PARENT OR ADOPTEE. If denied records on the grounds that the person is deceased, cite the following: "Davin v. U.S. Department of Justice, 60F.3d1043 (3rd Circuit 1995): Persons who are deceased have no privacy interest in non-disclosure of their identities."

10. FINDING DAD - REQUEST YOUR HOSPITAL RECORD OF BIRTH. Obtaining the hospital record of your birth may fill in the gap left by records that do not identify your father, or may address the question as to whether the person who had to be named as your "legal father" due to marriage was likely not your biological father. This is only feasible if you know your mother's name under which the hospital record would be filed at the time of your birth. You would need "the complete record for the mother and newborn, including: Admissions Record (which should indicate who paid–perhaps the father or other relative), doctor's and nurse's notes, newborn photo and/or footprint, delivery room record and discharge record." Do NOT indicate you are adopted, even if you know who's who, lest the Medical Records clerk denies you access.

11. APPLY FOR A PASSPORT. One technique some adoptees have used successfully for obtaining a copy of the original birth certificate that is otherwise denied them, is to apply for a passport. A birth certificate is required. But first request your Original Birth Certificate from the central (not local) office of Vital Records at the state's capital city, since that is the only place it will be, and state in your request that it is REQUIRED in order to apply for a passport. Enclose a copy of your passport application as proof that it is needed for that purpose and be sure to provide at the top of the letter your current name. Some have claimed a "Delayed Birth Record"(which adoptees' birth certificates are), rather than a "sealed record," as Vital Records can cross-reference your adoptive name with your birth name. Passport Services also requires "proof of adoption" and the only record that can provide such proof is your original birth certificate. Some Vital Records Clerk may actually send you your Original Birth Certificate–It's happened.

12. YOUR FOSTER CARE RECORDS ARE NOT SEALED RECORDS. Most adopted children are placed in foster care at least temporarily while awaiting completion of a home study for placement in their adoptive home. Many adoptees were in more than one foster home and for a longer period before adoption. One of the questions (#12) to ask when requesting non-identifying adoption information was whether you were in foster care and the names of your foster parents. Foster Care records are confidential but not sealed records and it is common for former foster kids to want to re-visit foster parents who treated them well, so you may be able to obtain your foster care records by written request with identification (a copy of your driver's license), and thereby discover your biological parents' names as well. Valid reasons would be (1) you wish to see and thank your foster family; (2) you wish to locate your siblings (whether or not you actually have sibs); (3) for any medical or health information which your doctor informed you would be helpful in diagnosing you

13. CHECK NON-PROFITS THAT MAY HAVE LOCATOR SERVICES. Mothers were formerly residents of Salvation Army Maternity Homes and Hospitals, and adoptees who were placed by agencies after birth at Salvation Army facilities have their own registries and search support groups online, including by state. You'll also find posts by searching Salvation Army mothers and adoptees at The Seeker = http://www.the-seeker.com/

14. BLACK MARKET ADOPTEES. Try "Black Market Adoptees' Registry" online at http://www.webring.org/ , Baby Brokers by state http://www.amfor.net/StolenBabies.html , and http://DOBSEARCH.com for date-of-birth search in cases where the name may be changed.

15. THE CONFIDENTIAL INTERMEDIARY SYSTEM.   The states have been amending laws by requiring use of a Confidential Intermediary (CI) for the purpose of opening the adoption file and locating the biological parent at the request of the adult adoptee and to communicate the adoptee's desire for information and/or contact. A CI can be appointed by a court or can be an adoption agency social worker, depending on state law.   CIs charge a non-refundable fee and are not permitted to divulge identifying information unless both parties agree. So there is a risk that the adoptee will gain nothing by paying a CI except the knowledge that either the CI did not locate the mother within the maximum hours the CI devotes to the task, assuming that an effort was made, or that the mother refused contact and any information including updated family medical information, thereby also preventing a search for the adoptee's biological father (if, for instance, the mother will not provide that information). Because what, how and for whom a CI performs this duty is entirely at the CI's discretion, AmFOR and this author encourages adoptees and parents to instead do their own searches, if possible, and to make their own direct contacts, rather than have a go-between attempt to deliver the messages and ask questions that both of you have had to wait years to communicate.   But sometimes this is not feasible.

In one case, AmFOR persuaded a Court appointed CI in Washington State to waive her fee for a Washington adoptee's biological grandmother who resided in California, because her daughter, the adoptee's biological mother, had died, and we provided proof to the court of the grandmother's low income (it never hurts to ask). The CI was able to locate the adoptee who then resided in neither Washington nor California, and he was glad to be found as he had no idea how to begin a search and could not afford a CI either. The CI charged only for the cost of long distance calls.   In another case, an adult adoptee incarcerated in Michigan was first denied even non-identifying information by Sister Joanne Ales, who headed Catholic Social Services of Macomb County. AmFOR donated the $60 fee by check, but Ales, who expressed disdain for all prisoners, returned AmFOR's check and required $250 from the prisoner to instead act as Confidential Intermediary, an obvious conflict of interest. Catholic Social Services in a different county in the same state of Michigan provided another incarcerated adoptee with his non-identifying information that even disclosed his father's first name.   For a current list of Confidential Intermediaries, contact the Court or Social Services, or the private agency involved, or Google "Confidential Intermediary" and the state name.

16. INCARCERATED ADOPTEES - are subject to the same state laws and rights for disclosure as other adoptees, regardless of crime for which convicted or the bias of the person holding the adoption file. If denied, inform the central office of Social Services and the Court of jurisdiction.

17. NATIVE AMERICAN ADOPTEE SEARCH RESOURCES. The 1978 Indian Child Welfare Act gives special preference in adoptions of Native American Children to the child's immediate relatives and tribe.   Yet there have been highly publicized court cases (such as the Dusten and Veronica Brown case, aka the "Baby Veronica" case), where a Native American child was adopted across state lines by a non-Indian couple over the objections of the Native American parent who wanted to raise her. Adult adoptees may find the Bureau of Indian Affairs helpful in identifying the tribe to which they belong. (The Mexican equivalent is The National Indian Institute.) However, the Bureau and the tribes must still abide by state law. So "how to" search information is still essential for Native Americans searching for family members separated by adoption.

18. INNOVATIVE AND BIZARRE SEARCH METHODS OF ADOPTEES AND PARENTS.

Birth indexes that cross-reference birth and adoptive names used to be easily accessed by card-carrying genealogists. Adoptees and parents have also reported resorting to more desperate actions, not advocated and which this book is designed to make unnecessary per their true stories, as follows: (1) A nationwide "search underground" has existed for many years whereby mothers have placed $2500 cash or some other amount in a Federal Express envelope addressed to open records activist, Jane Servadio, in Milford, Connecticut, who then puts them in touch with the anonymous underground searcher who provides the adoptee's identity and more; (2) An adoptee succeeded in cracking open his adopters' safe to find adoption papers; (3) a close friend of an adoptee went to the courthouse and requested to see the adoption file as if the adopter; when the Clerk asked for ID, the friend explained her name had been changed due to divorce and remarriage; the Clerk never blinked and the friend then provided the adoptee with her mother's name; (4) quickly accessing a Birth Index Book of the old printed type at courthouses when the Clerk is out on break; (5) peaking at one's adoption file that a social worker (sometimes intentionally) leaves on her desk while she's out of the room; (6) one of 8 siblings adopted separately and who learned their biological mother had died, determined where her grave was located and left a note in a bottle at the grave site. The reunited siblings erected a new tombstone for their mother inscribed "Mother's love brought us together –8 Little Orphans."

19. FAMILIES SEPARATED BY DIVORCE.

There are two kinds of child custody - legal custody and physical custody. A non-custodial parent, in law, is one with whom the child does not live but may have varying degrees of contact with their child or none at all for any number of reasons. Children separated by divorce also experience inequities of archaic state confidentiality" laws. While in cases of abuse, restraining orders and forced separation may be necessary, in most divorce situations, the parents' inability to get along imposes a punishment on the child who is loses contact with one of his parents.

If the custodial parent remarries, and the new spouse adopts the child, the same secrecy of records is imposed on a child in stepparent adoptions. Some of these children may know who there missing parent is but others do not if the separation occurred when they were very young. If it's the mother who has remarried, the child is usually given the stepfather's name. If it's the biological father who has remarried, the adopting stepmother may be listed as the mother at time of the stepchild's birth on an "amended" birth certificate and the child's original birth certificate is sealed (withheld) by law as in any adoption and the same adoption disclosure laws apply. Links for Child Custody Laws, by state can be found at http://singleparents.about.com/od/legalissues/a/custody_laws.htm, Resources on FACEBOOK for non-custodial parents include websites dealing with "parental alienation," "corrupt family courts," CPS Watch https://www.facebook.com/CPSWatch. CPS Watch National Hotline at 1-800-CPS-WATCH; and local helplines for child support problems are found at http://About.com which has links to every state's CUSTODY LAWS, as well as web pages with links for Fathers' Rights, Mothers Rights and "no fee legal help" for Single Parents.

Authorities in Washington state believe Joseph Kondro abducted, raped, and murdered as many as 70 young girls -- most still missing, their bodies hidden in the forests of the Pacific Northwest. But the serial killer would only confess to two of them in a plea bargain that saved him from Washington's Death Penalty. *In "KONDRO - The Untold Story of the Longview Serial Killer,"* by Lori Carangelo, the author explains how a whole community kept a deadly secret that enabled a killer to continue his evil deeds for many years, undetected.

Chapter 3:
MISSING and RUNAWAY CHILDREN

Since 1967, the federal government has operated a computerized National Crime Information Center (NCIC), originally used to catch criminals and recover missing property. In 1975 the Feds allowed local police to include skimpy information about missing persons. In 1982, Senator Hawkins proposed expanding the service to include listings by blood type, dental records, scars, and other information that would also help identify missing children. Since 1884, out of 945,000 annual entries into the FBI's NCIC database on missing persons, about 80% or 765,000 have been missing children.

The United Nations Special Rapporteur on Abducted Children determined, in the United Nations "Rights of the Child" Report that "the United States is the largest market for stolen children in the world, and California is the largest market for stolen children in the U.S." A child can sell for $80,000 or more for adoption, sex or pornography.

IF YOUR CHILD IS MISSING:

STEP 1 - LAW ENFORCEMENT, AMBER ALERT - America's Missing Broadcast Emergency Response. Immediately call your LOCAL law enforcement agency for an "AMBER ALERT" WITHIN 30 MINUTES from when you first perceived your child is missing. IT IS A MYTH THAT YOU MUST WAIT 24 HOURS BEFORE CONTACTING POLICE. Prompt notification to your local Amber Alert system has proven to rescue children.

If your child is missing from home, search through: closets, piles of laundry, in and under beds, inside large appliances, vehicles – including trunks, anywhere else that a child may crawl or hide. If your child cannot be found while shopping in a mall or large store, notify the store manager or security office. Then immediately call your local law enforcement agency. Many stores have a "Code Adam Plan" of action in place. Law Enforcement and child rescue teams urge parents to assemble an ID packet on each child each year with a color photo and fingerprints, and to teach a child to cause a commotion if a stranger grabs them, to have a child play and travel in groups, never leave a child alone in a car, and pick up a child from school and activities on time.

WHEN YOU CALL LAW ENFORCEMENT: Provide law enforcement with your child's name, date of birth, height, weight and descriptions of any other unique identifiers such as eyeglasses and braces. Tell them when you noticed your child was missing and what clothing he or she was wearing. Request law enforcement authorities immediately to enter your child's name and identifying information into the FBI's National Crime Information Center Missing Person File.

If your child is displaced during a disaster, immediately call your local law enforcement. Then fill out an Unaccompanied Minors Registry form. This tool lets NCMEC assist emergency management personnel on the ground in their efforts to reunite families during disasters such as hurricanes, tornadoes or terrorist attacks.

STEP 2 - NCMEC. Then call the National Center for Missing & Exploited Children at 1-800-THE-LOST (1-800-843-5678).

HOW NMEC HELPS

When you call NCMEC, a Call Center specialist will record information about your child. A NCMEC case management team will next work directly with your family and the law enforcement agency investigating your case. They will offer technical assistance tailored to your case to help ensure all available search and recovery methods are used. As appropriate NCMEC case management teams:

- Rapidly create and disseminate posters to help generate leads.
- Rapidly review, analyze and disseminate leads received on 1-800-THE-LOST (1-800-843-5678) to the investigating law enforcement agency.
- Communicate with federal agencies to provide services to assist in the location and recovery of missing children.
- Provide peer support, resources and empowerment from trained volunteers who have experienced a missing child incident in their own family.
- Provide families with access to referrals they may use to help process any emotional or counseling needs.

CHILD ABUSE. Consider whether the child may be hiding from someone in a position of trust and authority, such as a counselor or group leader, who could be secretly abusing the child, physically, emotionally or sexually. Runaways also hide from street gangs, drug dealers, parental and school authority, or due to problem relationships, pregnancy, etc.

TEEN RUNAWAYS. If a runaway is old enough to possess a driver's license, car, Social Security Number and other ID, and is likely to work at a particular job or has predictable habits, the runaway may be making a paper trail that can be followed and reveal addresses, contacts, and any aliases used. Older, more resourceful teens may become street survivors for a time but they can fall victim to drug dealers and prostitution. Check rescue shelters in suspect areas. CHILDREN OF THE NIGHT has rescued over 100,000 children from prostitution and offers a variety of services for them to have a good future - https://www.childrenofthenight.org/, and they have a 24-hour hotline at 1-800-551-1300. BOYSTOWN and GIRLSTOWN National Hotline counsels and informs via a variety of recorded options or via direct discussion with a counselor about problems and programs at 1-800-448-3000.

IDENTIFYING RECOVERED CHILDREN: Local police may provide free child ID cards and fingerprinting services. Know where your child's dental and medical x-rays are. There are websites offering "child safety products" such as ID cards and shoe tags and "child print ID kits." In cases where a child has been abducted as an infant and held for a long time, they may have no memory of their family. Computer enhanced age progression of a photo of the child can aid Law Enforcement and families still searching for a child who may be two or more years older. Private investigators can devote more time to current and "cold cases" of missing children and have developed inside resources.--See also National Missing and Unidentified System (NamUs) in Chapter 4, page 38.

STEP 3 - FACEBOOK AND HELPLINES. Posting a missing child's photo, description, date and time the child went missing (and from where, possible destinations if a parent abduction, etc) , on Facebook with your contact information and/or your local law enforcement phone number or Tipline, will build a network of people who are alerted or may actively help search for the child in specific areas as well as nationwide. If you can offer a reward leading to recovering the child, specify this, but have such leads filtered by Law Enforcement who can determine whether they are genuine.

Chapter 4:
MISSING ADULTS

An astounding 2,300 Americans are reported missing every day, including both adults and children. But only a tiny fraction of those are stereotypical abductions or kidnappings by a stranger. For example, the federal government counted 840,279 missing persons cases in 2001. All but about 50,000 were juveniles, classified as anyone younger than 18. The National Center for Missing Adults, (Let's Bring Them Home, http://lbth.org/ based in Phoenix), consistently tracks about 48,000 "active cases," says president Kym Pasqualini, although that number has been bumped up by nearly 11,000 reports of persons missing after devastating hurricanes. And slightly more than half of the 48,000—about 25,500—of the missing are men. About 4 out of 10 missing adults are White, 3 of 10 Black, and 2 of 10 Latino. Among missing adults, about one-sixth have psychiatric problems. Young men, people with drug or alcohol addictions, and elderly citizens suffering from dementia make up other significant subgroups of missing adults.

While Law Enforcement is the first step in getting help to find a missing child or adult, they may need convincing that the person is, in fact, missing, or may be working 30 cases at a time and so may not be able to produce leads quickly. This chapter provides self-help steps for attempting to locate missing adults, and simultaneous combination of resources is advised.

STEP 1: LAW ENFORCEMENT - If you are missing someone, call law enforcement immediately... time is of the utmost importance. With each tick of the clock when someone is missing, the odds of finding them is go down. It can sometimes be difficult to convince police that an adult has not voluntarily left and there may be a wait time before law enforcement will even take such a report or act on it. Consequently, you should provide sufficient reason to convince them that the person's absence is highly unusual, or that you have reason to believe they have Alzheimer's, are a danger to themselves or others, there may be foul play (such as if the person had received threats or been harassed before they went missing), or they disappeared without their car or purse. Websites are maintained by law enforcement such as the Department of Public Safety, Police Departments, Sheriff's Offices, and the FBI as public records in hope of helping to find people who are lost or missing.

STEP 2: LOCAL MEDIA - Your local TV News station(s) will inform you as to what is required before they can publicize that a person is missing. Media attention can be the quickest way to find someone, especially if the likely circumstances of the disappearance is known - such as a hiker known to have left for a hike in a specific area has not returned when expected, or someone who started on a trip, locally or at a distance, never reached their known destination or meeting at a scheduled time and can't be reached via their cell phone. Time can be critical for a missing person with a medical condition requiring daily treatment.

STEP 3: FACEBOOK and HELPLINES have been known to solve such cases by immediately alerting people to be on the lookout for the missing person, not only in the last known area seen but also by social media voluntarily networking nationwide. Local, National and International Organization and Helplines can be found by Googling key words such as "Missing Adult Organizations" or "Missing Adult Helplines"

SILVER ALERTS, for example, at http://www.ncmissingpersons.org/current-silver-alerts/ is a public notification system to broadcast information about missing persons – especially seniors with Alzheimer's Disease, dementia or other mental disabilities – in order to aid in their return.

THE NATIONAL MISSING AND UNIDENTIFIED PERSONS SYSTEM (NamUs) at http://www.namus.gov/ is a national centralized repository and resource center for missing persons and unidentified decedent records. NamUs is a free online system that can be searched by medical examiners, coroners, law enforcement officials and the general public from all over the country in hopes of resolving these cases.

The Missing Persons Database contains information about missing persons that can be entered by anyone; however before it appears as a case on NamUs, the information is verified. NamUs provides a user with a variety of resources, including the ability to print missing persons posters and receive free biometric collection and testing assistance. Other resources include links to state clearinghouses, medical examiner and coroner offices, law enforcement agencies, victim assistance groups and pertinent legislation. The Unidentified Persons Database contains information entered by medical examiners and coroners. Unidentified persons are people who have died and whose bodies have not been identified. Anyone can search this database using characteristics such as sex, race, distinct body features and even dental information. The newly added UnClaimed Persons database (UCP) contains information about deceased persons who have been identified by name, but for whom no next of kin or family member has been identified or located to claim the body for burial or other disposition. Only medical examiners and corners may enter cases in the UCP database. However, the database is searchable by the public using a missing person's name and year of birth. When a new missing persons or unidentified decedent case is entered into NamUs, the system automatically performs cross-matching comparisons between the databases, searching for matches or similarities between cases.

NamUs provides free DNA testing and other forensic services, such as anthropology and odontology assistance. NamUs' Missing Persons Database and Unidentified Persons Database are now available in Spanish.

Chapter 5: GENEALOGY SEARCHES

"In about four generations or so, about half the ancestry of the American population will be bogus," according to Attorney Brice M. Clagett, (in *"Adoption Laws Threaten the Death of Genealogy,"* National Genealogy Society Newsletter), because in all the states, adoptees' birth records name the adopters as the parents on the day of birth so their ancestry in public records is bogus.

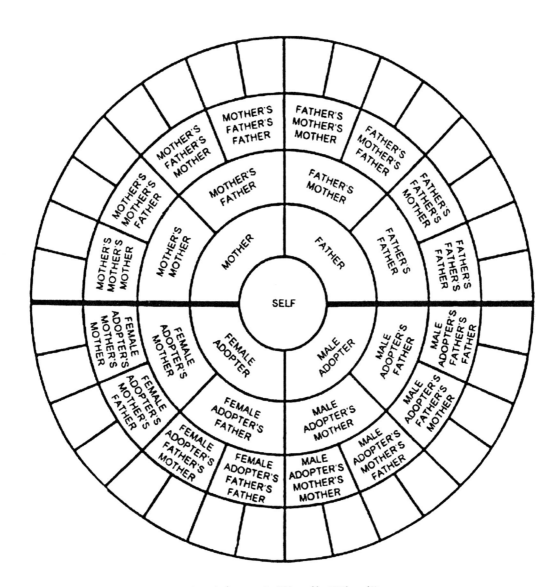

An Adoptee's "Family Wheel"

STEP 1: YOUR IMMEDIATE FAMILY. So great anyone's "natural need to know" our roots, it's not surprising that Ellis Island's Immigration Center's website had 8-million visitors in its first 8 hours of existence...and that the average person spent about $700 annually on genealogy (according to Elizabeth Bernstein, Wall Street Journal columnist in an interview on MSNBC back in 2001). The number of online researchers increase each year, as do their postings and software such as "Family Tree Maker-6th Edition." Tracing early Americans can be tricky. Few people in colonial times had three names but may be identified by their occupation without a comma: "John William Carpenter" in 1875 was probably John William - a carpenter. "John Henry Taylor" may have been John Henry - a tailor. Some wills and deeds were indexed by occupation and name. Many immigrants, or their children, "Americanized" their names, particularly movie stars. Benny Kubelski became Jack Benny.

A genealogy approach can be useful for adoptees who may know the name of a blood relative, living or deceased, on one side of his biological family, which can then lead to identities on both sides of the family.

STEP 2: THE MORMON CHURCH and ANCESTRY.com - a Treasure Trove of Worldwide Genealogy Records. The Mormon Church of Jesus Christ of Latter Day Saints has amassed the largest depository of worldwide genealogical records - over 600-million names, extracted from vital records worldwide. Genealogy is an important part of the LDS faith. Their genealogy library is headquartered in Salt Lake City, Utah, with Family History Center branches everywhere. Their microfilmed and recently digitized records are mostly "more than 50 years old" but pertain to everyone - not just Mormons - and many foreign births can be researched using not only their Family History Center branches but also their website at familysearch.org. To find a Family History Center in your area for browsing microfilm records free of charge, call 1-800-346-6044 or visit the web site. At www.familysearch.org you can check ancestral files, Census records, birth and death records, and the Social Security Death Index (you don't need to know the Social Security Number if the name is not too common).

STEP 3: OTHER OLINE RESOURCES:

INTERNET- **Ancestry.com** is the leading commercial web site for genealogy. Ancestry.com has over one million paid subscribers, and although they charge a fee to access their census records, passenger lists and other databases, the monthly fee starts at about $10 and also gives you access to Rootsweb.com, Genweb.com and other sites rich in genealogical content.

CLASSMATES.COM now enables viewers, without charge, to browse or upload for free entire high school yearbooks that are donated, and to upload your photo and profile. A membership fee allows you to contact other members.

FACEBOOK.COM still offers totally free registration to create your own Facebook page, to access pages by other individuals and groups. (for example "All Carangelos" is for anyone named Carangelo in Italy, the U.S. and worldwide), for social contacts as well as for tracking down living and ancestral relatives, further enabling anyone to grow their family tree with a click of a mouse. Family trees an be a simple keepsake album of photos of immediate relatives with their names and dates and places of birth and death for your children and grandchildren, but can also preserve the stories handed down through your family which make it interesting.

STEP 4: CASTLE GARDEN and ELLIS ISLAND. Castle Garden in New York's Battery served as America's first immigration station from 1830-1891 before Ellis Island opened in 1892. The 10 million immigrants who passed through Castle Garden's doors were mostly from Northern and Western Europe. Castle Garden's immigration records can be searched via its "one step" passenger lists by the person's name or ship name http://stevemorse.org/ellis/cg.html Find your ancestor by name on ship's manifest in one step, free at http://www.ellisisland.org/search/passSearch.asp - the ship's manifest is printable, if you right click at the top of the frame and select Print Preview, adjust for size and select Landscape instead of Portrait, though it may not capture the image edge to edge.

STEP 5: NATIONAL AND STATE ARCHIVES (NARA) FOR GENEALOGICAL RESEARCH. The National Archives and its many branches can be great resources for the genealogical researcher. There are also Archives branches by region. If you are unable to visit a National or Regional Archives in person, you can hire someone to do so, or simply write requesting the location of the information you seek and cost per page for copies. Types of records that can be browsed, rented or purchased from National Archives is explained at http://www.archives.gov/research/order/.

- NARA has genealogical workshops, and presentations at 7th and Pennsylvania Ave., NW, Washington, DC 20408, (202) 501-5400

- The Suitland Reference Branch of the National Archives (4205 Suitland Road, Suitland, Maryland, for personal visits; Washington, DC 20409 mailing address, (301) 763-7410) has more Federal records than any branch in the U.S. They include: Bureau of Land Management (1760-1890) land entry files and homesteads, War Relocation Authority (1940-1945) Japanese Americans Interned during WWII, Dept. Of State passports (1906-1925), U.S. District Court for D.C. (1800-1960), Patent and Trademark Office (1836-1919),

- The branch at College Park, Maryland, has no genealogical records, but has Nixon Presidential Materials, Center for Electronic Records, Cartographic Reference, Motion Picture, Sound and Video, and Still Picture collections.

- For records relating to military personnel in the National Archives, it's the National Records Center, 9700 Page Avenue, St. Louis, Missouri 63132 (Army: 314-538-4261; Navy, Coast Guard, Marines: 314-538-4141)

- To research American Indians and Alaska Natives (as early as 1774) (including individual ancestry), military records, and to order copies of records, these National Archives records can be accessed online at http://www.archives.gov/research/native-americans/index.html - or write to: The National Archives and Records Administration, 8601 Adelphi Road, College Park, MD 20740-6001. Their Customer Service line is happy to answer questions and to direct you to the right branch of the Archives for specific tribes at 1-866-272-6272

- RECORDS AVAILABLE TO SEARCH. Not only the National Archives, but also many major libraries throughout the United States have the following records as well as many other record types. These records can also be rented or purchased from Heritage Quest, Online at http://www.proquest.com/products-services/heritagequest.html, or at PO Box 329, Bountiful, Utah 84011-0329; (700) 760-2455.

Records are organized by Record Group, from smallest to largest:

- RECORD: a piece or item of information in any physical form (paper, photographic, motion picture tape, audio tape, computer tape, CD, etc.);
    - <u>Example</u>: A letter in a pension application file.
- FILE UNIT: Holds the records concerning the person, case, date or subject.
    - <u>Example</u>: Pension application file of an individual with supporting documents.
    - SERIES: Consist of File Units that deal with a particular subject, function or
    - activity, related by arrangement, source, use, physical form or action taken. <u>Example</u>: Series 1--Approved applications of wives; Series 2–Unapproved;
- SUB-GROUP: Contains 2 or more Series related by subject, activity and source; <u>Example</u>: Applications for same period, Sub-Groups Civil War and Later.
- RECORD GROUP: Sub-Groups are combined into Record Groups according to the origin of the Sub-Group material–often for the records of a Bureau. <u>Example</u>: Records of the Veterans Administration, Records Group 15.

YOUR FAMILY TREE.   Whether you decide to make a simple Family Tree of immediate family members on both the maternal and paternal side of your family, or a complex, in-depth Genealogy or Pedigree Chart, **the photos and especially the stories you discover and save will make it interesting to other family members and future generations.**

YOUR PEDIGREE CHART.   This is a more complex presentation of one's genealogy. The word "pedigree" is a corruption of the French "pied de grue" or crane's foot, because the typical lines and split lines (each split leading to different offspring of the one parent line) resemble the thin leg and foot of a crane.

Pedigrees use a standardized set of symbols, squares represent males and circles represent females. It should be noted that pedigree construction is family history, and as such details about an earlier generation may be uncertain as memories fade. If the sex of the person is unknown a diamond is used. Someone with the phenotype in question is represented by a filled-in (darker) symbol. Heterozygotes, when identifiable, are indicated by a shade dot inside a symbol or a half-filled symbol.

Relationships in a pedigree are shown as a series of lines. Parents are connected by a horizontal line, and a vertical line leads to their offspring. The offspring are connected by a horizontal sibship line and listed in birth order from left to right. If the offspring are twins then they will be connected by a triangle. If an offspring dies then its symbol will be crossed by a line. If the offspring is stillborn or aborted it is represented by a small triangle.

Each generation is identified by a Roman numeral (I, II, III, and so on), and each individual within the same generation is identified by an Arabic number (1, 2, 3, and so on). Analysis of the pedigree using the principles of Mendelian inheritance can determine whether a trait has a dominant or recessive pattern of inheritance. Pedigrees are often constructed after a family member afflicted with a genetic disorder has been identified. This individual, known as the proband, is indicated on the pedigree by an arrow.

If your research leads you to other countries, you can probably find genealogists who specialize in the country you'd like to have researched to find your ancestors and most often you won't be charged if the genealogist regards it as a hobby rather than a business. *The Ultimate Search Book – Worldwide Edition* includes resources in every state and 200 countries. Ancestry.com provides a simple fill-in-the blanks format for your name and name of one of your parents with any known information, then builds your Family Tree on both the paternal and maternal side of your family.

NATIONAL CENSUS. A Census of the population has been taken every 10 years since 1790 and can be a useful resource for tracing your family tree. Microfilm copies are available for the 1790-1880 schedules, for surviving fragments of the 1890 census, and for the 1900-1940 schedules. Almost all of the 1890 Census was destroyed by fire in 1921.

The remaining schedules for 1890 consist of small segments of the population of Perry County, AL; District of Columbia; Columbus, GA; Mound Township, IL; Rockford, MN; Jersey City, NJ; Eastchester and Brookhaven Township, NY; Cleveland and Gaston Counties, NC; Cincinnati and Wayne Township, OH; Jefferson Township, SD; and Ellis, Hood, Kauffman, Rusk and Trinity Counties, TX. The 1790-1840 schedules give the names of heads of household only; other family members are tallied unnamed by age and sex. For the 1850 and 1860 Censuses, separate schedules list slave owners and the age, sex and color (but not the name) of each slave, and the county of birth of each free person in the household. Additional information is included in each succeeding Census. The published censuses for 1790 are for Connecticut, Maine, Maryland, Massachusetts, New Hampshire, New York, North Carolina, and Vermont. Censuses for the remaining states–Delaware, Georgia, Kentucky, New Jersey, Tennessee and Virginia–were burned during the War of 1812. As a substitute, the federal government published names obtained from state censuses and tax lists, thereby listing over half the population of the state in 1790. Helpful in locating specific Census entries are the following unpublished indexes in the National Archives: 1810 Census – a card index for Virginia only; 1880 Census – a microfilm copy of a card index to entries for each household that included children under 10; 1890 Census – a card index to the 6,160 names of surviving schedules; 1900 Census – a microfilm copy of an index to heads of families; 1910 Census – a microfilm copy of an index to all heads of families in the following states: Alabama, Arkansas, California, Florida, Georgia, Illinois, Kansas, Kentucky, Louisiana, Michigan Mississippi, Missouri, North Carolina, Tennessee, Texas, Virginia, West Virginia. Also available on microfilm are the 1890 schedules of Union veterans and their widows in alphabetical order from Louisiana through Wyoming. Records are available relating to Indians who kept their tribal status, mostly 1830-1940. They include mainly Cherokee, Chickasaw, Choctaw and Creek, each of whom moved West during 1830-1846. Each entry on these lists usually contains the name of the head of the family, the number of persons in the family by age and sex, a description of the property owned before removal with the location of real property, and the dates of departure from the East and arrival in the West. The microfilm of the 1885 -1940 census rolls show each person in the family by their Indian or English name (or both), age, sex, relationship to head of family, sometimes their relationship to other enrolled Indians, and sometimes births and deaths during the year.

The Census Bureau, established in 1902, is now located at 4600 Silver Hill Road, Prince George's Country, Suitland, MD 20746; (301) 763-5636. For specific information from the last Census, check the site map at the bottom of their home page at https://www.census.gov/#

For in-depth statistical and anecdotal research about adoptees, donor offspring and their related issues, "THE ADOPTION AND DONOR CONCEPTION FACTBOOK" is available in both Kindle and print book format, or ask your local library to order it from Clearfield Books at Genealogical.com.

NATURALIZATION RECORDS. The Immigration and Naturalization Service (INS) has duplicate records of all naturalizations that occurred after September 26, 1906. Inquiries about citizenship granted after that date should be sent on a form available from INS district offices (address available from your local Postmaster).

GEN RING, PERSONAL FAMILY WEBSITES, MESSAGE BOARDS, GENEALOGY COLUMNS, NEWS GROUPS, DIRECTORIES, CHARTING SERVICES, COATS OF ARMS online can help you "branch out" in your search for your "roots."

- GenRing, web ring at http://hub.webring.org/hub/genring, has over 1,000 genealogy websites.
- Public Profiler's World Names website at http://worldnames.publicprofiler.org/ will map the frequency of your name around the world, free.
- Cyndi's List at http://CyndisList.com, has over 52,000 links in 100 categories, including free adoptee and parent reunion registries.
- Coats of Arms date back to the twelfth century. Frequently Asked Questions (and Answers) about Coats of Arms can be found at http://www.college-of-arms.gov.uk/resources/faqs

BOOKS AND RESEARCH. GENEALOGICAL PUBLISHING COMPANY INC. and CLEARFIELD COMPANY, at http://Genealogicial.com, publishes genealogy books and CDs. Whether you are just beginning to explore your family tree or are an experienced researcher looking for in-depth genealogy data, Genealogical.com can provide you with the resources you need. They publish over 2,000 genealogy books and CDs featuring colonial genealogy, Irish genealogy, immigration, royal ancestry, family history, and genealogy methods and sources. They publish the print version of *The Ultimate Search Book- Worldwide Edition* by this author, as well as "THE GENEALOGIST'S ADDRESS BOOK" by Elizabeth Petty Bentley, which has national and state addresses for archives, libraries, historical societies, genealogical societies, ethnic and religious organizations, and "HISTORY FOR GENEALOGISTS" by Judy Jacobson, which uses chronological time lines for finding and understanding your ancestors. Heritage Quest, at http://www.heritagequestonline.com/hqoweb/library/do/index is a publisher of genealogical books and materials and also offers a lending library. The aforementioned books are also available at public libraries, or can be if you ask the Acquisitions Librarian at your local public or university library to order them for both their Reference shelves and for check out.
(See also the Bibliography section of this book.)

Chapter 6:
DEBTORS; DEADBEAT PARENTS; HEIRS; CLASSMATES; OLD LOVES... or ANYONE

DEBTORS. Collection agencies in every city are able to pursue debtors for companies and individuals who are owed money, usually as result of being awarded a court judgment. Most do not charge up-front fees but will deduct a percentage, such as 50% of amounts if and when collected, according to a written agreement. The collections agency should offer the debtor the option of not having negative information placed on their credit report if they pay the debt promptly in full or in accordance with a monthly payment schedule.

If you want to try to collect on your own, you must first make a written demand for payment by certified return-receipt mail, stating the maximum time in which the debtor must pay you or make arrangement for payments. If you cannot collect what is owed you, the next step is to file a claim in Small Claims Court and obtain a judgment. If the debtor owns or may in the future own real estate, it's a good idea to have the County Recorder record the judgment so that a lien can be placed against the property. If the debtor is employed, you can hire the local authority who can serve the employer with an order to garnish the person's wages for the amount owed, or, if you know where the person banks, you can have the authority serve the bank with an Order to garnish the account. If the debtor has filed for bankruptcy, the bankruptcy court determines the priority of claims if there is money to pay them.

DEADBEAT PARENTS. There may be legitimate reasons for a parent to fall behind in child support payments, such as unemployment, which can be worked out by communicating, not avoiding the issue. But the parent will still owe any back child support payments missed, and in order to establish the parent's obligation, a court has to award a specific amount of child support to be paid until the child is of legal age. The child should have a Social Security Number and a child support payment account established. The District Attorney for the county in which the child support was incurred can sue the parent who owes child support and garnish their wages, place liens against property, and initiate legal prosecution to enforce court-ordered child support.

HEIRS. "Probate" is the legal determination by a Probate Court of the validity of a will. The Probate Court for the county in which the deceased maintained their "last legal residence" has jurisdiction and requires probate for estates over a certain amount (for instance, over $60,000).
The court does not search for heirs. A Legal Notice about the death and hearing must be published (usually by an attorney, administrator or executor) in a newspaper in the county of the last legal residence. A will usually designates an executor or administrator to carry out the deceased person's wishes. If a deceased relative or friend has named you as administrator or executor, you will have to locate any heirs if you don't already know where they are. If they are not listed in WhitePages.com or local directories, check Yellow Pages or online business directories for "Legal Services," "Locators" or similar listings for Heir Searchers who also advertise in the Martindale-Hubbell attorney directory at http://Martindale.com, since lawyers will hire them to find an heir. It is important that attempts to locate and legally notify heirs be documented. As when hiring a detective, check references.

CLASSMATES.   Classmates.com and Reunions.com make it easy to find a former classmate if she or she has added their name to those on the website as they can be found by browsing those listed. However, one must pay a membership fee in order to contact someone via Classmates.com messaging. Classmates.com and public libraries may have the high school yearbook for the year that the person you seek graduated. Forthcoming high school reunions and updates are posted.

OLD LOVES. People are often separated by circumstances such as war, distance, family or other relationships. We often hear about an older couple who haven't seen each other in decades and have re-kindled a past romance. They may have been married and divorced or widowed in the meantime, and may now be at a place in their lives where the relationship can be fulfilling.   This book provides all the ways that you can find anyone anywhere, even without knowing their current name to start. If you had originally met while in school, Classmates.com may provide their current whereabouts and a means for contact.   Depending on how much you knew and remember about the person, you might find them at the same job or business, or through mutual friends.   You may both, by coincidence, both be on Facebook, or a dating website such as Match.com, or OurTime.com for singles who are 50+. As with any search for someone you haven't seen in a long time, one must be respectful of the other person's current situation and whether or not they are interested in meeting again.

Chapter 7:
STARTING YOUR OWN SEARCH BUSINESS

While it's been the policy of this author and her organization, Americans For Open Records (AmFOR), to not charge fees for search assistance, charging reasonable fees for one's work and actual expenses is certainly acceptable. There are two types of search businesses. One is the result of enjoying doing research to solve a case, just as one would have satisfaction from solving any puzzle. The other type results from a deep sense or moral conviction that "the system" is inadequate to serve the needs of those you can help with your services. It's not illegal to search for one's family, but in the case of adoptee and parent searches, the system creates roadblocks to prevent people from accessing records in which they are named, and from the freedom to choose whether to associate. Consequently, the people within the system sell them the information and contact with biological family members. In order to decide whether a search business would be of interest to you, complete a search – your own or a friend's – and become familiar with your local registrar's and other public records offices and their publicly accessed computers. Another way to find your niche is to work for a private investigator or an attorney who needs someone to do "skip tracing" and property searches on an hourly or flat fee basis (for instance, so much per skip trace). The job of searching property files on computer or in file drawers at a county tax assessor's office, and civil and criminal records and dockets at courthouses or online, can be tedious, but the end result can be satisfying. After requiring experience as a skip tracer, researcher or searcher, you will have a better idea whether you want to spend your time on the same repetitive tasks, or are flexible enough to enjoy the challenge that each new case may present.

TIPS FOR DEVELOPING A SUCCESSFUL SEARCH BUSINESS.
STEP 1: TEST THE MARKET. After you've decided on a good name for your business; filed your fictitious name statement; obtained a business license; set up a business account; bought a computer and reliable Internet access; found out what others are charging for the same services and priced yours competitively; created a web page about your business with photos; made some inexpensive business cards that list your services, phone number, mailing address, email address and website, don't spend a lot of money for ads while just waiting for the phone to ring. Find and fill the needs of local attorneys, security companies, collections agencies, bail bondsmen, preferably by face to face contact and hand them your card. Look for individuals and adoptee groups on Facebook whose pages and newsfeeds state they are looking for someone.
STEP 2: NOTIFY OTHERS YOU EXIST – PROMOTE YOUR BUSINESS WITH A VIDEO TAPE featuring a human interest case you've solved and offering your help with other cases. Next upload the video to You Tube, being sure your phone number is prominently displayed.
STEP 3: BUILD YOUR REFERENCE LIBRARY. "BIZ-OPS 2013: STARTING, BUYING & SELLING BUSINESSES" by Dr. Stanley S. Reyburn offers sound advice and resources at http://www.amazon.com/dp/B00BKA4DD4

BIBLIOGRAPHY

Austin, Linda Tollet, *"Babies For Sale: The Tennessee Children's Home."*
    Greenwood Press, (1993)

Bentley, Elizabeth Petty, *"The Genealogist's Address Book - 6th Edition,"* (812 pages),
    Genealogical Publishing Company, (2009)

Bertrand, Neal, *"From Cradle to Grave: Journey of the Louisiana Orphan Train Riders,"*
    Cypress Cove Publishing, (2014)

Block, William , *"Advanced Private Investigation,"* Information Today, (2001)

Blockson, Charles, *"Black Genealogy,"* Black Classic Press, (1991)

Brodzinsky, David M., *"Being Adopted The Lifelong Search for Self,"* Doubleday, (1992)

Burton, Bob, *"Bail Enforcer: The Advanced Bounty Hunter,"* Paladin Press, (1990)

Campbell, Lee H., PhD, *"Cast Off: They Called Us Dangerous Women,"* (2014); and
    "Stow Away: They Told Me to Forget," CreateSource Independent Publishing, (2013)

Carp, E. Wayne, *"Jean Paton and the Struggle to Reform American Adoption,"* University of
    Michigan Press, (2014)

Chatelain, Maurice, *"Our Ancestors Came From Outer Space,"* Dell Publishing,(1991)

Clagett, Brice M., *"The Death of Genealogy,"* National Genealogical Society Newsletter,
    (February 1990)

Cox, Susan Soon-Keum, *"Voices From Another Place: A Collection of Works From a
    Generation Born in Korea and Adopted to Other Countries,"* Yeong & Yeong, (1999)

Department of Justice, *"A Family Resource Guide on International Parental Kidnapping,"*
    CreateSpace Independent Platform, (2012)

Eldridge, Sherry, *"Twenty Things Adopted Kids Wished Their Adoptive Parents Knew,"*
    Dell Books, (1999)

Fessler, Ann, *"The Girls Who Went Away,"* Penguin Books, (2000)

Gauthreaux, Alan G., *"Italian Louisiana: History, Heritage and Tradition,"*
    The History Press, (2014)

Greenwood, Val D., *"A Researcher's Guide to American Genealogy,"* 3rd Edition, Genealogical
    Publishing Company, (2013)

Griffith, Keith C., *"The Right To Know Who You Are,"* Katherine Kinbell Pubisher, (1992)

Hoffman. Michael, *"They Were White and They Were Slaves: The Untold History of the
    Enslavement of Whites in Early America,"* Independent History, (1993)

Jacobson, Judy, *"History for Genealogists: Using Chronological Time Lines to Find and
    Understand Your Ancestors,"* Clearfield Company for Genealogical Publishing, (2009)

Katz, William Loren, *"The Black West: A Documentary and Pictorial History of the African
    American Role in the Western Expansion of the United States,"* Touchstone, (1996)

Krantz, Les, and Chris Smith, *"The Unofficial Census,"* Arcade Publishing, (2003)

Lifton, Betty, *"Journey of the Adopted Self: A Quest for Wholeness,"* Basic Books, (1995)

McGilvrey, Valerie, *"Skip Trace Secrets: Dirty Little Tricks Skip Tracers Use,"* CreateSpace
    Independent Platform, (2013)

Melanson, Yvette, and Claire Safran, *"Looking for Lost Bird: A Jewish Woman's Discovery of
    Her Navajo Roots,"* Harper Perennial, (2000)

Moreno, Barry, *"Children of Ellis Island,"* Arcadia Publishing, (2003)

Newton, Nancy, *"Primal Wound: Understanding Your Adopted Child,"* Gateway Press, (2003)

Price, Gary, and Chris Sherman, *"The Invisible Web: Uncovering Information Sources Search Engines Can't See,"* Information Today, (2001)

Rose, James M., PhD, and Alice Eichholz, PhD, *"Black Genesis,"* Genealogical Publishing Company, (2008)

Smolenyah, Megan, *"Who Do You Think You Are?: The Essential Guide to Tracing Your Family History,"* Penguin Books, (2010)

Simon, Rita J., *"In Their Own Voices: Transracial Adoptees Tell Their Stories,"* Columbia University Press (2000)

Smith, Franklin Carter, and Emily Ann Croom, *"A Genealogist's Guide to Discovering Your African American Ancestors,"* Genealogical Publishing, (2005)

Solinger, Rickie, *"Beggars and Choosers: How the Politics of Choice Shapes Adoption, Abortion and Welfare in the United States"* Holt and Wang, (2002); and *"Wake Up Little Susie: Single Pregnancy and Race Before Roe v. Wade",* 2nd Edition, Routledge, (2000)

Thomas, Gordon, *"Enslaved: The Chilling Modern-Day Abduction and Trafficking of Men, Women and Children,"* Pharos Books, (1991)

Von Danekni, Erich, *"Chariots of the Gods,"* Berkeley Press, (1990); and *"History is Wrong,"* New Page Books, (2012)

Wenzel, Rosemary, *"Tracing Your Jewish Ancestors - Second Edition: A Guide for Family and Historians,"* Pen and Sword (2014)

Werner, Emma E., *"Passage to America: Oral Histories of Child Immigrants from Ellis Island,"* Potomac Books, (2009)

Wheeler, Joan M., *"Forbidden Family,"* Trafford Publishing, (2009)

RESOURCES AND WEBSITES

ADOPTEE, BIRTHPARENT, SIBLING SEARCH &/OR SUPPORT, PIs (See also REUNION REGISTRIES)

ALMA SOCIETY (Adoptees Liberty Movement Association) - http://www.almasociety.org/

AMERICAN ADOPTION CONGRESS (AAC) http://americanadoptioncongress.org

AMERICANS FOR OPEN RECORDS (AmFOR) - http://AmFOR.net

BASTARD NATION (BN) http://bastards.org

CONCERNED UNITED BIRTHPARENTS (CUB) - http://info@CuBirthparents.org

EMERGENCY, LIFE OR DEATH SEARCH (Volunteers available sporadically) http://ties-search.org email: l TIES@absnw.com

PRIVATE INVESTIGATION NETWORK P.I. MALL - http://www.pimall.com/

SEARCH ANGELS (Free) at THE SEEKER http://www.the-seeker.com/angels.htm ON FACEBOOK https://www.facebook.com/pages/Adoption-Free-Search-Angels/156749834387458 AND OTHERS http://adoption.com

ADOPTION DISCLOSURE LAWS

THE ADOPTION AND DONOR CONCEPTION FACTBOOK (e-book and print edition) - http://AmFOR.net/AdoptionFactbook

BASTARD NATION http://bastards.org/activism/access.htm

ADOPTION and FOSTER CARE INFORMATION

ACCESS PRESS http://AccessPressBooks.com

ADOPTION & DONOR CONCEPTION FACTBOOK, THE http://AmFOR.net/AdoptionFactbook

AMERICANS FOR OPEN RECORDS (AmFOR) [Huge, Free Public Information site - Right Panel links lists pages alphabetically] http://AmFOR.net http://AmFOR.net/adoption

CHILD WELFARE INFORMATION GATEWAY (Federal Government website) https://www.childwelfare.gov/

CHOSEN CHILDREN (A Documentary) http://AmFOR.net/ChosenChildren

ADOPTION REFORM ACTIVISTS & ABOLITION GROUPS

ADOPTION ACTIVISTS THINKING OUTSIDE THE BOX https://facebook.com/groups/942900502390600/1021862751161041/?ref=notif&notif_t=group_activity

ADOPTIVE PARENTS FOR OPEN RECORDS & AGAINST ADOPTION http://Facebook.com/Anti-AdoptionAdopters

AMERICANS FOR OPEN RECORDS (AmFOR) http://AmFOR.net http://AmFOR.net//abolishadoption

BASTARD NATION
http://www.bastards.org/
FACEBOOK GROUPS
https://www.facebook.com/groups/anti.adoption/
?notif_t=group_r2j_approved
http://Facebook.com/AbolishAdoption
https://facebook.com/groups/35338433808147

POUND PUP LEGACY
http://PoundPupLegacy.org

DNA/GENETIC TESTING AND MATCHING SERVICES

ANCESTRY.COM ($99 Autosomal and
Y-Chromosome) -http://Ancestry.com

CABRI DONOR GAMETE ARCHIVE
(Male & Female, X/Y Chromosone DNA)
[Pro: Connects half-siblings/donors for
offspring using X/Y chromosome testing;
Con: Only can connect siblings of the same sex,
and females must have mother tested]
http://cabrimed.org/donorconceivedservices.jsp

DNA DATABASES
http://isogg.org/wiki/DNA_databases

DNA TESTS ($99. Autosomal) -
23andme.com

FAMILY TREE DNA ($60 Autosomal) -
http://FamilyTreeDNA.com

HOME DNA
https://.homedna.com/paternity_test.php?gclid=
CPHqnq2H7rsCFcJ0QgodqH0AKg

TESTING BY MAIL
http://gtldna.com/RelationshipTesting/DNAPate
rnity-Testing.htm

UPLOAD DNA TEST RESULTS
(only from 23andMe) -
http://GEDMatch.com

Y-SEARCH Y-DNA PUBLIC DATABASE
(Male only, Y chromosome DNA)
Pro: Can identify paternal genetic surname,
giving male offspring an idea as to their

biological father's possible last name
Con: Because of infidelity/secret adoption and
donor-conception in direct line, genetic surname
may not be same as biological father's surname
http://Ysearch.org

DONOR OFFSPRING, SIBLING RESOURCES - REGISTRIES, FORUMS, SOCIAL NETWORKS

AMERICAN ASSOCIATION OF TISSUE
BANKS
http://aatb.org

AMERICAN SOCIETY FOR
REPRODUCTIVE MEDICINE (ASRM)
http://asrm.org

CHICAGO WOMEN'S HEALTH CENTER
(BANK)
http://chicagowomenshealthcenter.org

CRYOBANK's SIBLING REGISTRY
http://sibling-registry.com/howtoregister.cfm
https://nwcryobank.com/sign-in/?message=sign-
inrequired

DONOR CHILDREN
http://donorchildren.com
http://donorchildren.com/sample-
page/getstarted

DONOR CONCEIVED REGISTER (UK)
http://donorconceivedregister.org.uk

DONOR CONCEPTION (Pre-1991)
http://fairfaxcryobank.com

DONORLINK (UK) (National Voluntary
Info Exchange and Contact Register
http://ukdonorlink.org.uk

DONOR, OFFSPRING, PARENT, SIBLING
REGISTRY (Totally Free; Worldwide;
sponsored by AmFOR)
http://AmFOR.net/DonorOffspring

DONOR OFFSPRING GROUP
http://DonorOffspring.com

DONOR OFFSPRING HEALTH PAGE
http://donoroffspringhealth.com

DONOR OFFSPRING RESEARCH PROJECT
(participation invited)
http://donorfamilyresearch.com

DONOR SIBLING REGISTRY (DSR)
(Fee for access; Wendy Kramer)
http://donorsiblingregistry.com

EVERYTHING SURROGACY -
Directories for Surrogacy Agencies, Egg
Donation Services, Attorneys, IVF
http://everythingsurrogacy.com

FAIRFAX CRYOBANK REGISTRIES
http://fairfaxcryobank.com

MIDWEST SPERM BANK
http://midwestspermbank.com

PEOPLE CONCEIVED BY ARTIFICIAL
INSEMINATION (PCVAI)
http://health.groups.yahoo.com/group/
PCVA

SEARCHING FOR MY SPERM DONOR
FATHER
(Australia/US/UK/Canada profiles)
http://www.searchingformyspermdonorfather.or
g/country/Canada/

SPERM DONOR GROUP
http://health.groups.yahoo.com/group/Sperm
Donors/?yguid=3457069
http://www.donorsiblinggroups.com/Donor_
Sibling_Group_Registr.php

KNOWN DONOR REGISTRY
http://KnownDonorRegistry.com

Y CONNECTIONS REGISTRY (Australia) -
https://www.donorconnections.com
/

[See also DNA/GENETC TESTING AND
MATCHING SERVICES]

GENEALOGY RESOURCES

ANCESTRY.com
http://Ancestry.com

ROOTSWEB
http://wc.rootsweb.ancestry.com/cgibin/
igm.cgi

BIOGRAPHIES FOR GENEALOGY
http://geneabios.com/

CYNDI'S LIST
http://cyndislist.com/

FAMILY TREE BUILDER
http://myheritage.com

FIND A GRAVE at
INTERNMENT.net
http://interment.net/

GENEALOGICAL PUBLISHING
(FOR SPECIFIC SUBJECT, COUNTRY)
http://Genealogical.com

GENWEB
U.S. GENWEB PROJECT
http://usgenweb.org/

WORLDGENWEB
http:/worldgenweb.org/countryindex.html

INTERNATIONAL GENEALOGICAL
INDEX
https://familysearch.org/search?PAGE=igi/s
earch_IGI.asp

SOCIAL SECURITY DEATH INDEX
http://genealogy.about.com/od/free_genealo
gy/a/ssdi.htm

SORTED BY NAME
http://sortedbyname.com/index.html

MISSING CHILDREN

NATIONAL CENTER FOR MISSING &
EXPLOITED CHILDREN (NCMEC)
http://missingkids.com

PRISONER LOCATOR

PRISONER LOCATOR, BY STATE (Free)
http://ancdestorhunt.com/prison)search.htm

CALIFORNIA PRISONER LOCATOR
http://inmatelocator.cdcr.cagov (Free)

PUBLIC RECORDS DATABASE
http://searchsystems.net

REUNION REGISTRIES

ADOPTION DATABASE - REGISTRIES
https://adoptiondatabase.quickbase.com/db/b
bqm94vvd

INTERNATIONAL SOUNDEX REUNION
REGISTRY (ISRR) - (Free)
http://isrr.org; http://isrr,org/Register.html

MILITARY SEARCH
http://searchmil.com

NAME SEARCH DIRECTORIES
PEOPLE SEARCH, DOB SEARCH,
REVERSE LOOKUPS,
BIRTH INDEXES. DEATH IDEX

http://WhitePages.com
http://AnyWho.com
http://411.com
http://SearchGateway.com (Free)
http://PeopleSearch.com (Fees apply)
http://Intelius.com (Fees apply)
http://Facebook.com
http://MySpace.com

http://Classmates.com
http://reunions,com
http://DOBSEARCH.com
BIRTH INDEXES -
Visit you local FAMILY HISTORY
CENTER to view microfilm Birth Indexes

DEATH INDEX
http://rootweb,com
http://ancestry.com/search

RANCH HANDS DATABASE
http://searches.rootsweb,com

SUBJECT SEARCH ONLINE.
LIBRARIAN'S INDEX TO THE
INTERNET
http://sunsite.berkeley.edu/InternetIndex

ULTIMATE SEARCH BOOK, THE -
(WORLDWIDE EDITION and
U.S. EDITION, e-book & print edition)
http://AmFOR.net/UltimateSearch

WORLDWIDE PHONE DIRECTORIES
http://www.phonebookoftheworld

INDEX

ADDENDUM
BIRTH CERTIFICATES AND RELATED FORMS

(1)   **My Hospital Issued Birth Certificate** (Connecticut)

(2)   **My State Health Department Issued Birth** (Connecticut)

(3)   **My State Vital Records Issued Birth Certificate** (Connecticut)

(4)   **My Granddaughter's Short Form** (Coupon Size) **Certificate** (Connecticut)

(5)   **My Son's Original** (True) **Birth Certificate** *Biological Parents on Date of His Birth* (CT)

(6)   **My Son's Amended** (Falsified) **Birth Certificate**
        His Adoptive Parents As Parents On Date Of His Birth (CT)

(7)   **Adoptee's Original Army Base Hospital Issued Provided To Adoptee,**
        Blocked, As "Non-Identifying Information" (Hawaii)

(8)   **Adoption Decree**, Unblocked (Washington State)

(9)   **Adoption Certificate** (Unofficial, created by an adoptive mother)

(10)   **Waiver Of Confidentiality For "Birth" Mothers** (Generic for any state)

(11)   **Waiver Of Confidentiality For Siblings** (California)

(12)   **Consent For Contact For "Birth" Mother Or Adoptee (California)**

(13)   **International Soundex Reunion Registry** (ISRR) Regstration Form (Page 1)

(14)   **International Soundex Reunion Registry** (ISRR) Registration Form (Page 2)

(15)   **Request To Waive Court Fees** (California)

(16)   **U.S. State Department Issued Apostille Birth** (Alabama, California, Washington Examples)

(17)   **Hospital Record Of Newborn's Footprints Thumb And Finger Prints**

(18)   **Certified Nurse Midwife (Cnm) Home Birth & Midwife License** (Illinois)

(19)   **County Issued Birth Certificate** (Cook County, Illinois)

(20)   **City Issued Birth Certificate** (Chicago, Illinois)

(21)   **Catholic Birth And Baptism Certificate**

(22)   **Jewish Birth Certificate With Child's Hebrew & Circumcision Certificate** (New York)

(23)   **Mormon Birth Certificate From Record At Chihuahua, Mexico** (Salt Lake City, Utah)

(24)   **"Sex Not Specified" Birth Certificate** (Australia)

(25)   **No Gender of** (Lgbt) **Parents Birth Certificate** (California)

(26)   **3 Parent** (Lgbt) **Birth Certificate** (Florida)

The Hospital of Saint Raphael

Certificate of Birth

This Certifies that _Lorraine Caranuto_

was born to _Alfred Betheume and Inez Caranuto_

in this Hospital at _7:45 P.m. Tuesday_

the _____ day of _____ A. D. 19____

In Witness Whereof the said Hospital has

caused this Certificate to be signed by its duly authorized

officer and its Official Seal to be hereunto affixed.

Sister Rose Alice

Hospital Administrator

Attending Physician

(1) MY HOSPITAL ISSUED BIRTH CERTIFICATE
(Connecticut)

STATE OF CONNECTICUT   DEPARTMENT OF HEALTH

Notice of Registration of Birth

This is to certify that

Lorraine Carangelo   ~~Street~~

was born___April 3,____19 45 in Hospital of St.Raphael
                                              New Haven, Conn.
Father's name   Alfred B.Carangelo

Mother's maiden name   Anna Dolceacqua

The full record of this birth has been carefully filed and is preserved in the
archives of the State of Connecticut

Stanley H. Osborn . M.D.   Joseph D. Linde M.D.
Commissioner of Health   Health Officer.

EVERY MOTHER IS ENTITLED TO A "NOTICE OF REGISTRATION OF BIRTH" OF HER CHILD.

O. V. S. 52A (4-44) 20M

(2) MY DEPARTMENT OF HEALTH BIRTH REGISTRATION
(Connecticut)

CONNECTICUT STATE DEPARTMENT OF HEALTH

Certificate of
Birth

1. Place of Birth:
a. County   New Haven, Conn
b. City or Town   New Haven, Conn
c. Name of Hospital
   or institution   St.Raphael's Hosp.
   Note: If not in hospital or institution,
   give street No. or location
d. Length of mother's stay before
   delivery: in hospital or institution   1 day
   In this community   17 yrs.
3. Full name of child   Lorraine Carangelo
4. Date of birth   Apr. 3, 1945
   month   day   year
5. Sex   female

2. Usual residence of mother:
a. State   Conn
b. County   New Haven, Conn
c. City or town   New Haven, Conn
d. Street No.   92 Carmel St.
6. Twin or triplet?
   If so, born 1st, 2nd, 3rd?
7. Number months of pregnancy   9

FATHER OF CHILD
8. Full name   Alfred B. Carangelo
   Residence   New Haven, Conn.
9. Race   white   10. Age   40
11. Birthplace   New Haven, Conn
    City or town   State or foreign country
12. Usual
    occupation   High Standard
13. Place of
    occupation   -
14. Social Security Number

MOTHER OF CHILD
15. Full maiden name   Anna Dolceacqua
16. Race   white   17. Age   30
18. Birthplace   New York City, New York
    City or town   State or foreign country
19. Usual
    occupation   housewife
20. Place of
    occupation   -
21. Social Security Number   -

22. Other Children born to this mother:
   (a) How many other children of this mother
       are now living?   0
   (b) How many other children were born
       alive but are now dead?   0
   (c) How many children were born
       dead?   0

23. Mother's mailing address for registration
    notice   Above

    Was blood test made?   yes
    Date   2-45
    If not made, give reason   -

24. I hereby certify that I attended the birth of this child; who was born alive at the hour of
    3:59 a.M. on the date above stated and that the information given was furnished by
    related to this child as   mother

25. Date on which given name added on supple-
    mental report
    By   Registrar

    Attendant's own signature
    S. Capecelatro,   M.D.
    Specify if physician, midwife, or other
    Date Signed   4-3-45
    Address   New Haven, Conn

Form O-VS 16 Rev. (7-44) 40M

THE SEAL OF THE STATE DEPARTMENT OF HEALTH SERVICES IS AFFIXED TO CERTIFY THAT
THE ABOVE IS A TRUE COPY OF A RECORD FILED WITH THE DEPARTMENT OF HEALTH
SERVICES PURSUANT TO THE PROVISIONS OF THE GENERAL STATUTES OF CONNECTICUT.

Douglas S. Lloyd, M.D.
Commissioner of Health Services

SEP 1 2 1983

Registrar of Vital Records

(3) MY STATE ISSUED BIRTH CERTIFICATE
(Connecticut)

CERTIFICATION OF BIRTH

STATE OF CONNECTICUT
DEPARTMENT OF PUBLIC HEALTH

Vital Records Section, Hartford, Connecticut, U.S.A.

Registration No. 106-91-16272

Name RACHEL ELIZABETH SOLLECITO

Date of Birth May 23, 1991   Sex Female

Place of Birth   New Britain, CT

Reg. Date 6/4/1991   Date Issued 12/8/2010

This is a True Certification of Name and Birth Facts
as Recorded in this Office

By

Local Register of Vital Statistics

Town of   New Britain

STATE OF CONNECTICUT

(4) MY GRANDDAUGHTER'S SHORT FORM (COUPON SIZE) BIRTH CERTIFICATE
(Connecticut)

CONNECTICUT STATE DEPARTMENT OF HEALTH

Public Health Statistics Section — Hartford, Connecticut, U.S.A.

Certificate of Birth

REGISTRATION NO. 106-68 **46563**

1. PLACE OF BIRTH: (a) State of Connecticut		2. USUAL RESIDENCE OF MOTHER: (a) State **Conn.**		
(b) County	(c) Town	(b) County	(c) Town	(d) Is Residence Inside a City or Borough Limits?
New Haven	New Haven	New Haven	Hamden	Yes ☐ No ☐ If Yes, name City or Borough
(d) Name of Hospital or Institution (If not in a hospital or institution, give Street No. or location)		(e) Street Number (If rural, give location)		
Hospital of St. Raphael		201 Augur Street		

3. CHILD'S NAME (Type or Print)	(First) Richard	(Middle)	(Last) Marotti	4. DATE OF BIRTH (Month) (Day) (Year) December 17, 1968
5. SEX Male	6. (a) THIS BIRTH Single ☒ Twin ☐ Triplet ☐	(b) IF TWIN OR TRIPLET, WAS CHILD BORN 1st ☐ 2nd ☐ 3rd ☐	7. (a) LENGTH OF PREGNANCY COMPLETED 58 WEEKS	(b) WEIGHT AT BIRTH 6 lb. 15 oz.

FATHER OF CHILD

8. FULL NAME Anthony P. Marotti

9. RESIDENCE 201 Augur Street, Hamden, Conn.

10. RACE White   11. AGE AT TIME OF THIS BIRTH 26

12. BIRTHPLACE (City or town) New Haven   (State or foreign country) Conn.

13. USUAL OCCUPATION Drill press operator

14. INDUSTRY OR BUSINESS Unknown

15. (a) WAS BLOOD TEST MADE? (Yes or No) Yes   (b) Date of test 6-11-68

(c) If blood test not made, reason why not

MOTHER OF CHILD

11. FULL MAIDEN NAME Lorraine Carangelo

16. RACE White   17. AGE AT TIME OF THIS BIRTH 23

18. BIRTHPLACE (City or town) New Haven   (State or foreign country) Conn.

19. PREVIOUS PREGNANCY HISTORY OF THIS MOTHER (Do NOT include this birth)
(a) How many other children of this mother are now living? 0
(b) How many other children were born alive but are now dead? 1
(c) How many children were born dead? (Products of conception, fetuses, born dead at ANY time after conception) 0

21. MOTHER'S MAILING ADDRESS 201 Augur Street, Hamden, Conn.

22. I HEREBY CERTIFY that I attended the birth of this child who was born alive at the hour of 1:12a m. on the date above stated and that the information given was furnished by **Lorraine Marotti** related to this child as **Mother**

23. (a) ATTENDANT'S OWN SIGNATURE *George H. Bonner M.D.* George L. Bonner, M.D.   (b) Date Signed 12-16-68

(c) Address 111 Sherman Ave, New Haven, Conn 06511

24. DATE ON WHICH GIVEN NAME ADDED   By _____ REGISTRAR

THIS CERTIFICATE RECEIVED FOR RECORD ON DEC 23 1968   REGISTRAR

By *Gaetano Masella*

Form VS-2

I certify that this is a true transcript of the information in this office.

Michael V. Lynch

Michael V. Lynch, Registrar
Carol Longobardi, Deputy Registrar
Maria DeGaetano, Ass't Registrar

Dated at New Haven, Connecticut, U.S.A., this **27** day of **NOVEMBER**, 1996

NOT VALID WITHOUT SEAL

(5) MY SON'S ORIGINAL (TRUE) BIRTH CERTIFICATE NAMING HIS PARENTS ON DATE OF HIS BIRTH
(Connecticut)

CONNECTICUT STATE DEPARTMENT OF HEALTH

Public Health Statistics Section — Hartford, Connecticut 06115, U. S. A.

46563

Certificate of Birth

1. PLACE OF BIRTH: (a) State of Connecticut		2. USUAL RESIDENCE OF MOTHER: (a) State Connecticut		
(b) County	(c) Town	(b) County	(c) Town	(d) Is Residence Inside a City or Borough Limits?
New Haven	New Haven	New Haven	Meriden	
(d) Name of Hospital or Institution (If not in hospital or institution, give Street No. or location)		(e) Street Number (If rural, give location)		Yes ☐ No ☐ If Yes, name City or Borough
Hospital of Saint Raphael		35 Sylvan Avenue		

3. CHILD'S NAME (First) (Middle) (Last) (Type or Print)			4. DATE (Month) (Day) (Year) OF BIRTH
Thomas William Schafrick			December 17, 1968

5. SEX	6. (a) THIS BIRTH	(b) If TWIN or TRIPLET, WAS CHILD BORN	7. (a) LENGTH OF PREGNANCY (b) WEIGHT AT
Male	Single ☒ Twin ☐ Triplet ☐	1ST ☐ 2ND ☐ 3RD ☐	COMPLETED WEEKS BIRTH 6 15 oz.

FATHER OF CHILD	MOTHER OF CHILD
8. FULL NAME	15. FULL MAIDEN NAME
William Arthur Schafrick	Lois Edna Waller
9. RESIDENCE	16. RACE / 17. AGE AT TIME OF THIS BIRTH
Meriden, Connecticut	White / 27
10. RACE / 11. AGE AT TIME OF THIS BIRTH	18. BIRTHPLACE (City or town) (State or foreign country)
White / 29	Connecticut
12. BIRTHPLACE (City or town) (State or Foreign country)	19. PREVIOUS PREGNANCY HISTORY OF THIS MOTHER
Connecticut	(a) How many other children of this mother are now living? 0
13. USUAL OCCUPATION	(b) How many other children were born alive but are now dead? 0
Landscaper	(Do NOT include this birth) (c) How many children were born dead? 0
14. INDUSTRY OR BUSINESS	(Products of conception, fetuses, born dead at ANY time after conception)
Landscaping	
20. (a) WAS BLOOD TEST MADE? (Yes or No) — (b) Date of test —	21. MOTHER'S MAILING ADDRESS 35 Sylvan Avenue Meriden, Connecticut
(c) If blood test not made, reason why not —	

22. I HEREBY CERTIFY that I attended the birth of this child who was born alive at the hour of 1:12a m. on the date above stated and

that the information given was furnished by _____ related to this child as _____

23. (a) ATTENDANT'S OWN SIGNATURE	(b) Date Signed
George A. Bonner, M.D.	December 16, 1968
(c) Address	
111 Sherman Avenue, New Haven, Connecticut	

24. DATE ON WHICH GIVEN NAME ADDED	REGISTRAR By
THIS CERTIFICATE RECEIVED FOR RECORD ON December 23, 1968	REGISTRAR By Gaetano Masella

Form V.S. 33-8   4-70 5M

I certify that this is a true transcript of the information in this office.

Michael V. Lynch

Michael V. Lynch, Registrar
Carol Longobardi, Deputy Registrar
Maria DeGaetano, Ass't Registrar

Dated at New Haven, Connecticut, U.S.A., this 27 day of NOVEMBER, 1996

NOT VALID WITHOUT SEAL

**(6) MY SON'S AMENDED (FALSIFIED) BIRTH CERTIFICATE
NAMING HIS ADOPTIVE PARENTS AS HIS PARENTS ON DATE OF HIS BIRTH
(Connecticut)**

STATE OF HAWAII   **CERTIFICATE OF LIVE BIRTH**   DEPARTMENT OF HEALTH

FILE NUMBER 1 ███ **63** ███

1a. Child's First Name (Type or print)	1b. Middle Name	1c. Last Name
ALAN	███	███

2. Sex	3. This Birth	4. If Twin or Triplet, Was Child Born	5a. Birth Date	Month	Day	Year	5b. Hour
Male	Single ☒ Twin ☐ Triplet ☐	1st ☐ 2nd ☐ 3rd ☐		███ber	███	1963	█:47 A M.

6a. Place of Birth: City, Town or Rural Location	6b. Island
Honolulu	Oahu

6c. Name of Hospital or Institution (If not in hospital or institution, give street address)	6d. Is Place of Birth Inside City or Town Limits? If no, give judicial district
U. S. Army Tripler General Hospital	Yes ☒ No ☐

7a. Usual Residence of Mother: City, Town or Rural Location	7b. Island	7c. County and State or Foreign Country
Wahiawa	Oahu	Honolulu, Hawaii

7d. Street Address	7e. Is Residence Inside City or Town Limits? If no, give judicial district
███ Drive	Yes ☒ No ☐

7f. Mother's Mailing Address	7g. Is Residence on a Farm or Plantation?
	Yes ☐ No ☒

8. Full Name of Father	9. Race of Father
███	Caucasian

10. Age of Father	11. Birthplace (Island, State or Foreign Country)	12a. Usual Occupation	12b. Kind of Business or Industry
24	███	Officer	U. S. Army

13. Full Maiden Name of Mother	14. Race of Mother
███	Caucasian

15. Age of Mother	16. Birthplace (Island, State or Foreign Country)	17a. Type of Occupation Outside Home During Pregnancy	17b. Date Last Worked
22	███	School Teacher	10 Apr 63

I certify that the above stated information is true and correct to the best of my knowledge.	18a. Signature of Parent or Other Informant		18b. Date of Signature
	███	Parent ☒ Other ☐	6 Sept 63

I hereby certify that this child was born alive on the date and hour stated above.	19a. Signature of Attendant		19b. Date of Signature
	███ CAPT, MC, USA	M.D. ☒ D.O. ☐ Midwife ☐ Other ☐	6 Sept 63

20. Date Accepted by Local Reg.	21. Signature of Local Registrar	22. Date Accepted by Reg. General
6 Sept 63	███ LT COL, MSC, USA	SEP 10 1963

23. Evidence for Delayed Filing or Alteration

---

(7) ADOPTEE'S ORIGINAL (ARMY BASE HOSPITAL) BIRTH CERTIFICATE PROVIDED TO THE ADOPTEE, BLOCKED, AS "NON-IDENTIFYNG INFORMATON" (Hawaii)

FILED
AUG 2 0 2004
JoAnne McBride, Clerk, Clark Co.

SUPERIOR COURT OF THE STATE OF WASHINGTON FOR CLARK COUNTY

In the Matter of the Adoption

of

CHANCHAL

        A Minor Child.

NO. 04 5 00424 6

DECREE FOR ADOPTION

THIS MATTER having come on regularly this day on the Petition of SCOTT JACKSON DONWERTH and MAYLA DAWN DONWERTH, husband and wife, for the adoption of CHANCHAL, and the Petitioners and the above named minor child appearing in person and by their attorney, and it appearing that Children's Hope International, the agency appointed by the Court to prepare the Postplacement Report, has filed said report, and the Court being fully advised in the premises, and having heard the evidence, and findings of fact and conclusions of law having been previously entered by the Court.

ADOPTION SUMMARY

1   The full original name of the person being adopted is CHANCHAL

2   The new name of the person being adopted is AYANNA CHANCHAL DONWERTH

3   The adoptee's actual date of birth is May 7, 2003

4   The adoptee's place of birth is the Country of India

1 – DECREE FOR ADOPTION

Law Office of David R. Duncan
Post Office Box 1734
Vancouver, Washington 98668
(360) 816-1498
Fax (360) 816-1499

(8) ADOPTION DECREE (UNBLOCKED)
(Washington state)

Certificate of Adoption

This is to Certify that

MELISSIA ANNE GOODHEART

Has Been Formally Adopted

Into the Allman Family by the Mother Linda

and is Entitled to all the Rights and Privileges there to as One of Her Kids

ON THIS 1ST DAY OF JULY 2005

Linda J. Allman
Foster Mother

Philip E. Abbott
Senior Administrator

(9) ADOPTION CERTIFICATE (UNOFFICIAL)
Created by an Adoptive Mother

Dated: _____

TO (Address it to Child and Family Services or similar public adoption agency, or to private
    adoption agency or attorney, where adoption was finalized and adoption file is held)

REF: My Name in full _____

    Relinquished Child's Name at birth _____

    Child's Date and Place of Birth _____

    Relinquished/Placed for Adoption (on or about): _____

RE: NOTICE AND WAIVER OF CONFIDENTIALITY - TO ALL CONCERNED

I, _____, hereby formally request that this Notice and of my Waiver
of Confidentiality not guaranteed to me by any laws or agencies in the state of _____
and/or copies hereof be immediately placed in all records and files pertaining to my above-referenced
adoption. This Waiver of Confidentiality applies to all court records, hospital and other records of birth and
medical history, and anything that may be considered to be identifying information. I hereby also request
non-identifying information about my relinquished child and would like to know whether there is any
correspondence in the record intended for me or for my relinquished child.

The effects of this Waiver extend only to my "birth" child and/or my "birth" child's legal representatives.
The following information may be released in full to the aforementioned parties. My name in full, my current
address and phone number (shown below), any and all medical records that may be in file.

This Waiver gives my full and legal permission to release my present identity and contact information as
shown below and this letter is to remain in effect unless and until formally revoked by me in writing.

Please acknowledge receipt of my Waiver of Confidentiality in writing for my record.

Thank you,

_____
(Signature)

_____
(Printed Name in Full)

_____
(Current Address)

_____

_____
(Current Phone Number)

(10) WAIVER OF CONFIDENTIALITY FOR "BIRTH" MOTHERS
(Generic for Any State)

WAIVER OF RIGHTS TO CONFIDENTIALITY FOR SIBLINGS

INSTRUCTIONS:

1. Please complete entire form.
2. **This form must be witnessed by a representative of the California Department of Social Services (CDSS) or a California (CA) adoption agency licensed by the CDSS, or notarized by a Notary Public.*** If the signing of this form is witnessed by the CDSS or a California licensed adoption agency representative, photo identification of the person signing must be obtained and noted on this form. **THIS FORM WILL BE RETURNED TO YOU IF IT IS NOT WITNESSED OR NOTARIZED.**
3. The waiver may be sent directly to the CA licensed adoption agency which handled the adoption, if known, or to the CDSS' Central Office: CDSS, Adoptions Support Unit, 744 P Street, M.S. 3-31, Sacramento, CA, 95814. If the adoption was an agency adoption, the waiver will be returned to you with the name and address of the adoption agency that handled the adoption so that you may send it directly to that adoption agency for processing.

DESIGNATE ONE - I AM THE:

☐ **ADOPTEE (age 18 or older)**

☐ **SIBLING (age 18 or older)**
Attach copy of birth certificate

☐ **STEP-SIBLING (age 18 or older)** Attach copy of birth certificate **AND** copy of marriage certificate or divorce decree for marriage between birth parent and step-parent.

PART A. *To be completed by adoptee/sibling signing consent*

☐ ADULT ADOPTEE:

By signing this form, I voluntarily and knowingly waive my rights to the confidentiality of personal information known or contained in the files of the CDSS or the CA licensed adoption agency and give my consent to the CDSS or the CA licensed adoption agency to disclose my name and address to my sibling so he/she may contact me.

☐ ADULT SIBLING:

By signing this form, I voluntarily and knowingly waive my rights to the confidentiality of personal information known or contained in the files of the CDSS or the CA licensed adoption agency and give my consent to the CDSS or the CA licensed adoption agency to disclose my name and address to my adopted sibling so that he/she may contact me.

I realize that both of the designated persons must sign a Waiver before the CDSS or the CA licensed adoption agency may disclose identifying information and that signing this Waiver does not necessarily ensure that a contact will be made. The sibling must also comply with all other provisions of Family Code Section 9205.

I certify that to the best of my knowledge, I am an adoptee or sibling of an adoptee. I understand that I should keep the CDSS or the CA licensed adoption agency informed of my current name, address, and phone number in writing.

I understand that I have the right to revoke this waiver at any time by notifying the CDSS or the CA licensed adoption agency in writing.

I understand that if the CDSS or the CA licensed adoption agency has not received a Waiver from each designated person, I may file a petition in the Superior Court to appoint a confidential intermediary to search for the other party to attempt to obtain a Waiver.

NAME (PLEASE PRINT)		BIRTHDATE	OTHER NAME(S) BY WHICH ADOPTEE/SIBLING HAS BEEN KNOWN	
STREET ADDRESS	CITY	STATE	ZIP CODE	TELEPHONE NUMBER ( )
SIGNATURE			DATE	

PART B. **To be completed by a representative of the CDSS or a CA licensed adoption agency. If Part B or C is completed, do not complete Part D.**

SIGNATURE OF THE CDSS OR A CA LICENSED ADOPTION AGENCY REPRESENTATIVE	DATE	TELEPHONE NUMBER ( )
AGENCY/DEPARTMENT NAME	ADDRESS	

IDENTIFICATION OF ADULT ADOPTEE OR ADULT SIBLING (SPECIFY, I.E., DRIVER'S LICENSE, PASSPORT, ETC.)

PART C. ☐ *Check if notarized signature has been previously submitted to the CDSS or a CA licensed adoption agency.*

PART D. *To be completed by a Notary Public ONLY if Part B or C is not completed.*

State of _____)

County of _____)

On _____ before me, _____ , a Notary Public,

personally appeared _____ ,proved to me on the basis of satisfactory evidence to be
NAME OF ADULT ADOPTEE/ADOPTEE'S SIBLING

the person whose name is subscribed to the within instrument and acknowledged to me that he/she executed the same in his/her authorized capacity, and that by his/her signature on the instrument the person, or the entity upon behalf of which the person acted, executed the instrument.

I certify under PENALTY OF PERJURY under the laws of the State of California that the foregoing paragraph is true and correct.

WITNESS my hand and official seal.

_____ (Seal)
Signature

*Definition of Notary Public: A Notary Public is a public officer authorized by law to certify documents and to confirm your identity. Notaries may be located at most banks and credit unions or listed in the yellow pages of your local phone directory.

AD 904A (3/08) **SEE REVERSE SIDE**

(11) WAIVER OF CONFIDENTIALITY FOR SIBLINGS
(California)

CONSENT FOR CONTACT

Distribution Instructions:
Original: Agency/Department
Copy: Person Signing

1. Please complete both sides of this form.

2. **This form must be witnessed by either a representative of the California Department of Social Services (CDSS) or a California (CA) adoption agency licensed by CDSS, or notarized by a Notary Public.*** If the signing of this form is witnessed by a CDSS or adoption agency representative, photo identification of the person signing must be obtained and noted on this form. **THIS FORM WILL BE RETURNED TO YOU IF IT IS NOT WITNESSED OR NOTARIZED**

DESIGNATE ONE:
I am the

☐ Birth Parent

☐ Adult Adoptee
(age 18 or older)

PART A. *To be completed by person signing consent*

☐ BIRTH PARENT:

By signing this form, I voluntarily give my consent to the CDSS or licensed adoption agency to disclose my name and address to my adult biological child who was adopted so he/she may contact me.

☐ ADULT ADOPTEE:

By signing this form, I voluntarily give my consent to the CDSS or licensed adoption agency to disclose my name and address to my birth parent(s) so he/she may contact me.

I understand that the CDSS does not provide search services to locate birth parents or adoptees and that these parties must contact CDSS or the licensed adoption agency to request a Consent for Contact (AD 904) form.

I understand that the birth parent(s) and the adoptee must sign a consent before CDSS or the licensed adoption agency may disclose identifying information and that signing this consent does not necessarily ensure that a contact will be made pursuant to Family Code Section 9204. I understand that the law prohibits CDSS or the licensed adoption agency from soliciting, directly or indirectly, the execution of such a consent.

I understand that I should keep the CDSS or the licensed adoption agency informed of my current name and address.

I understand I have the right to rescind this consent at any time by notifying CDSS or the licensed adoption agency in writing.

NAME (PLEASE PRINT)	OTHER NAME(S) BY WHICH I HAVE BEEN KNOWN

STREET ADDRESS	CITY	STATE	ZIP CODE	TELEPHONE NUMBER ( )

SIGNATURE	DATE

PART B. *To be completed by a representative of CDSS or a CA licensed adoption agency. If Part B or C is completed, do not complete Part D.*

SIGNATURE OF CDSS /ADOPTION AGENCY REPRESENTATIVE	DATE	TELEPHONE NUMBER ( )

AGENCY/DEPARTMENT NAME	ADDRESS

IDENTIFICATION OF BIRTH PARENT/ADULT ADOPTEE (SPECIFY, I.E., DRIVER'S LICENSE, PASSPORT, ETC.)

PART C. ☐ *Check if applicable. Notarized signature has been previously submitted to CDSS or a CA licensed adoption agency.*

PART D. *To be completed by a Notary Public ONLY IF Part B or C is not completed.*

COMPLETED BY Notary Public

The Notary Public must staple the Acknowledgement document to this form and sign and date below.

SIGNATURE OF NOTARY	DATE

*Definition of Notary Public: A Notary Public is a public officer authorized by law to certify documents and to confirm your identity. Notaries may be located at most banks and credit unions or listed in the yellow pages of your local phone directory.

(12) CONSENT FOR CONTACT FOR "BIRTH" PARENT OR ADOPTEE
(California)

RN		S	DOB		FOR OFFICE USE ONLY		I
STAFF					COUNTRY	STATE	II

MAIL TO: ISRR, P.O. BOX 371179, LAS VEGAS, NV 89137

Official Registration Form
-- Confidential --

COMPLETE BOTH PAGES of this form, use BLACK Ink, THEN PRINT, SIGN & MAIL.

Please read the guidelines on page 4. This will help you fill out the form correctly

This registration is my FIRST ENTRY ☐   an UPDATE ☐

I AM THE: ADOPTEE/CHILD ☐   BIRTH PARENT ☐   BIRTH SIBLING ☐   OTHER: (explain)_____

PRESENT NAME:_____   REFERRED BY:_____

ADDRESS:_____ CITY:_____ STATE:_____ ZIP:_____

TELEPHONE NUMBER(S)   HOME: (____)____-_____   SOCIAL SECURITY #:_____-____-_____

WORK: (____)____-_____   E-MAIL:_____

Information About the CHILD   MALE ☐   FEMALE ☐

BIRTH DATE (Month/Day/Year)_____ TIME_____ AM ☐ PM ☐ BIRTH WEIGHT_____ lb ____ oz

HOSPITAL (Birth Place)_____ ATTENDING PHYSICIAN (Or Other)_____

CITY OF BIRTH_____ COUNTY_____ STATE_____ COUNTRY_____

NAME GIVEN AT BIRTH_____

NAME GIVEN AT ADOPTION_____

ADOPTIVE PARENT'S NAMES_____

BIRTH CERTIFICATE #'s – File #_____ Registrar #_____

IF THIS WAS A PLURAL BIRTH (Twins/Triplets, etc.), How many MALES?_____ How many FEMALES?_____

Were they separated by adoption?   YES ☐   NO ☐   Their Name(s)_____

COURT OF JURISDICTION_____ CITY_____ STATE_____

ATTORNEY OF RECORD_____ DATE OF FINAL DECREE_____

This adoption was -- PRIVATE ☐   BY AN AGENCY ☐   SOCIAL WORKER/INTERMEDIARY_____

NAME OF PLACEMENT AGENCY_____ CITY_____ STATE_____

INTERNATIONAL SOUNDEX REUNION REGISTRY, Inc.

(13) INTERNATIONAL SOUNDEX REUNION REGISTRY(ISRR.org)
REGISTRATION FORM, page 1

Information About the BIRTH PARENTS (at time of separation):

Including all info you know is very important. It helps ISRR determine relationships. Please enter everything you have. Update ISRR when you acquire additional data. Get your non-identifying info from state or agency. Click on "Get More Info" at www.isrr.net for guidelines.

	Birth Mother	Birth Father
NAME(S)		
Maiden Name		
Used At time of Birth		
Signed on Relinquishment/Consent		
BIRTH DATE	Age At Birth	Age At Birth
BIRTH PLACE		
MARITAL STATUS		
RELIGION		
EDUCATION		
OCCUPATION		
MILITARY BRANCH		
ANCESTRY		
DESCRIPTION	HEIGHT WEIGHT HAIR EYES	HEIGHT WEIGHT HAIR EYES
OTHER CHILDREN		
PARENT'S NAMES		

REMARKS: (use a separate sheet if needed)

- To help ISRR use contributions wisely, please keep your address, phone number & email current and notify ISRR if you are reunited -

I, the undersigned, hereby give my permission to the International Soundex Reunion Registry to release this vital information to the person(s) for whom this search is conducted. I understand this permission is necessary to activate registration, facilitate contact and for verification of identity, and my relationship to that person or persons.

X Signature Required_____Date_____

ALTERNATIVE ADDRESS AND/OR PHONE _____

"THIS IS YOUR REGISTRY - YOUR CONTRIBUTION IS TAX DEDUCTIBLE"

Registration remains free because of the generosity of those we serve - ISRR is a non-profit 501(c)3 tax exempt corporation

© 1993-2009 International Soundex Reunion Registry   WE LOOK FORWARD TO SERVING YOU!

PLEASE PRINT, SIGN AND MAIL THIS FORM TO:
ISRR, P.O. Box 371179, Las Vegas, NV 89137

ISRR will notify you only when a match is made. If you wish confirmation that your form has been received, include a self-addressed stamped envelope with this registration or update. Please do not send anything that requires signatures, or for volunteers to wait in line at the post office. Thank You.

(14) INTERNATIONAL SOUNDEX REUNION REGISTRY (ISRR.org) REGISTRATION FORM, page 2

73

Request to Waive Court Fees

Clerk stamps date here when form is filed.

If you are getting public benefits, are a low-income person, or do not have enough income to pay for household's basic needs and your court fees, you may use this form to ask the court to waive all or part of your court fees. The court may order you to answer questions about your finances. If the court waives the fees, you may still have to pay later if:
- You cannot give the court proof of your eligibility,
- Your financial situation improves during this case, or
- You settle your civil case for **$10,000** or more. The trial court that waives your fees will have a lien on any such settlement in the amount of the waived fees and costs. The court may also charge you any collection costs.

Fill in court name and street address:

Superior Court of California, County of

(1) Your Information *(person asking the court to waive the fees):*
Name: _____
Street or mailing address: _____
City: _____ State: ___ Zip: _____
Phone number: _____

Fill in case number and name:

Case Number:

(2) Your Job, if you have one *(job title):* _____
Name of employer: _____
Employer's address: _____

Case Name:

(3) Your Lawyer, if you have one *(name, firm or affiliation, address, phone number, and State Bar number):*
_____
_____

a. The lawyer has agreed to advance all or a portion of your fees or costs *(check one):* Yes ☐ No ☐
b. *(If yes, your lawyer must sign here)* Lawyer's signature: _____
If your lawyer is not providing legal-aid type services based on your low income, you may have to go to a hearing to explain why you are asking the court to waive the fees.

(4) What court's fees or costs are you asking to be waived?
☐ Superior Court (See *Information Sheet on Waiver of Superior Court Fees and Costs* (form FW-001-INFO).)
☐ Supreme Court, Court of Appeal, or Appellate Division of Superior Court (See *Information Sheet on Waiver of Appellate Court Fees* (form APP-015/FW-015-INFO).)

(5) Why are you asking the court to waive your court fees?
a. ☐ I receive *(check all that apply):* ☐ Medi-Cal ☐ Food Stamps ☐ SSI ☐ SSP ☐ County Relief/General Assistance ☐ IHSS (In-Home Supportive Services) ☐ CalWORKS or Tribal TANF (Tribal Temporary Assistance for Needy Families) ☐ CAPI (Cash Assistance Program for Aged, Blind and Disabled)
b. ☐ My gross monthly household income (before deductions for taxes) is less than the amount listed below. *(If you check 5b, you must fill out 7, 8, and 9 on page 2 of this form.)*

Family Size	Family Income	Family Size	Family Income	Family Size	Family Income	*If more than 6 people*
1	$1,215.63	3	$2,061.46	5	$2,907.30	*at home, add $422.92*
2	$1,638.55	4	$2,484.38	6	$3,330.21	*for each extra person.*

c. ☐ I do not have enough income to pay for my household's basic needs *and* the court fees. I ask the court to *(check one):* ☐ waive all court fees ☐ waive some of the court fees ☐ let me make payments over time *(Explain):* _____ *(If you check 5c, you must fill out page 2.)*

(6) ☐ Check here if you asked the court to waive your court fees for this case in the last six months. *(If your previous request is reasonably available, please attach it to this form and check here:)* ☐

I declare under penalty of perjury under the laws of the State of California that the information I have provided on this form and all attachments is true and correct.
Date: _____

▶

_____   _____
Print your name here   *Sign here*

Judicial Council of California, www.courts.ca.gov
Revised February 20, 2014, Mandatory Form
Government Code, § 68633 Cal. Rules of Court,
rules 3.51, 8.26, and 8.818

Request to Waive Court Fees

(15) REQUEST TO WAIVE COURT FEES
(California)

APOSTILLE BIRTH CERTIFICATES

An "apostille" is a form of authentication issued to documents for use in countries that participate in the Hague Convention of 1961. A list of countries that accept apostilles is provided by the US State Department.

If the country of intended use does not participate in the **Hague Convention** , documents being sent to that country can be "authenticated" or "certified".

The Office of the Secretary of State provides apostille and authentication service to U.S. citizens and foreign nationals on documents that will be used overseas. Types of documents include corporate documents such as company bylaws and articles of incorporation, power of attorney, diplomas, transcripts, letters relating to degrees, marital status, references and job certifications, home studies, deeds of assignments, distributorship agreements, papers for adoption purposes, etc. The U.S. State Department provides general information about document authentications and apostilles under the Hague Convention of 1961.

(16) U.S. STATE DEPARTMENT ISSUED APOSTILLE BIRTH CERTIFICATES
(Alabama, California, Washington state)

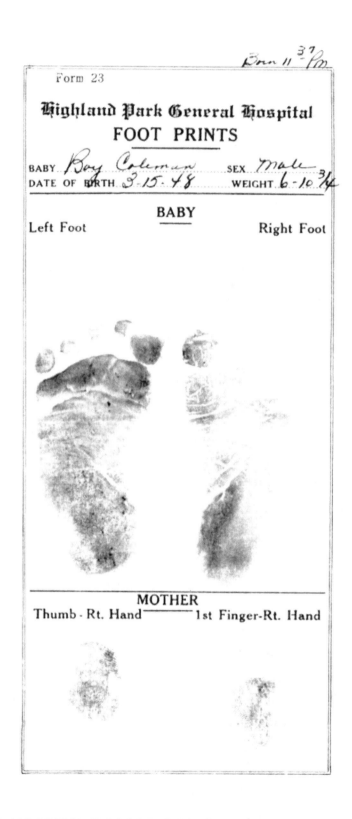

**(17) HOSPITAL RECORD OF NEWBORN'S FOOTPRINTS
WITH MOTHER'S THUMB AND FINGER PRINTS**

At 2:55 am on January 31st, 2012

Benjamin Joel T

was Born At Home in Pasco
to Paula T & John T

weighing 7 lbs & 5 oz. measuring 20 in long.

Birth attended by:
Sarah & Katie
caught by Daddy
and after the birth...
Fran Wilcox, CNM
Kat Frolich, assistant

NUMBER

STATE OF ILLINOIS
DEPARTMENT OF
REGISTRATION AND EDUCATION

This is to Certify

That _Rudolph W Stone_
is duly registered and entitled to practice as a

LICENSED MIDWIFE

under the provisions of An Act to revise the law in relation to the practice of the art of treating human ailments.

This License is revocable for the causes specified in the law and must be conspicuously displayed in the place of business or legal residence of the holder thereof.

In Witness Whereof, the Director of Registration and Education has hereunto affixed his hand and the seal of the said Department this 10th day of March 1923.

**THIS IS A
DUPLICATE
CERTIFICATE**

Original License dated August 31, 1916

Attest

(18) CERTIFIED NURSE MIDWIFE (CNM) HOME BIRTH CERTIFICATE
& MIDWIFE LICENSE
(Illinois)

The physician or midwife (when in attendance), or the parent or householder should immediately send this certificate accurately filled out to the County Clerk of the County in which the birth takes place. Penalty for not making report within 30 days, fine of $10 to $100, or imprisonment in jail for 30 days, or both.

STATE OF ILLINOIS,
Cook County.

REPORT OF BIRTH.

VITAL STATISTICS DEPARTMENT—COUNTY CLERK'S OFFICE.

1. † Full Name of Child ...... *Ralph Thompson*
2. Sex ...... *M* ...... Race or Color (if not of the white race) ......
3. Number of Child of this Mother ...... *2* ...... How many now living (in all) *2*
4. Date of this Birth ...... *July 15 – 1913*
5. Place of Birth, No. *2645* Street *N. Avers Ave* City Village Town
6. Residence of Mother, No. *Same* Street *"*
7. Place of Birth TOWN STATE OR COUNTRY AGE OF
   a. Father ...... *Norway* *27*
   b. Mother ...... *Ill* *24*
8. Full Name of Mother ...... *Dena Thompson*
9. Maiden Name of Mother ...... *C. Vallgren*
10. Full Name of Father ...... *Axel M. Thompson*
11. Occupation of Father ...... *Painter*
12. Name and Address of Nurse or Attendant (if any) ......
    Reported by ...... *J. M. Geary, M.D.* M. D. or Midwife
    Date ...... 19 ...... Residence *4421 Kemual Ave* Telephone *901 Ber*

* Still-births should be reported on a separate blank form.
† The baptismal or christian name of child should be certified, if possible, when this certificate is made, and should, in any case, be reported to the County Clerk within a year.
‡ In case of more than one child at a birth, a SEPARATE RETURN must be made for each, and the number of each, in order of birth, stated.

(19) COUNTY ISSUED BIRTH CERTIFICATE
(Cook County, Illinois)

(20) CITY ISSUED BIRTH CERTIFICATE
(Chicago, Illinois)

BIRth and Baptismal certificate

BIRth and Baptismal certificate

Diocese of _Killaloe_   Parish of _Birr_

On examination of the Register of Baptisms of above Parish I certify that

according to it _Thomas Tobin_

was born on _8_ day of _March 1863_, and was

baptised according to the Rites of the Catholic Church on_____day of

_____in the Church of _St. Brendans_

Birr by the Rev. _J. Scanlan cc._

Parents _John Tobin_

Ellen Halloran

Sponsors _James Keiffe_

Mary Tobin

Confirmed_____ Married_____

Signed _Fr. J. Scanlan_ P.P._____

Given this _6_ day of _November_ 19 _86_ at _____

Birr

LS.

VERITAS CO. LTD., DUBLIN

(21) CATHOLIC BIRTH AND BAPTISMAL CERTIFICATE

**(22) JEWISH BIRTH CERTIFICATE WITH CHILD'S HEBREW NAME
AND CIRCUMCISION CERTIFICATE (New York)**

Church of Jesus Christ of Latter Day Saints

Salt Lake City, Utah, _August 3, 1942_

This Certifies that according to the Records of the Church of Jesus Christ of Latter Day Saints -

_____GRANT G. BROWN_____

was born on the _eighteenth day of September, Eighteen Hundred Ninety-nine_

at _Juarez, Chih., Mexico_

Father's name _Orson P. Brown_

Mother's maiden name _Jane Galbraith_

Joseph Fielding Smith

Historian of the Church and ex officio Custodian of its Records

(Taken from Juares Stake, Morelos Ward Record of Children blessed, book 2118 entry 46). Entered on Records in the year 1899 by O. P. Brown.

CERTIFICATE OF BIRTH

(23) MORMON BIRTH CERTIFICATE
FROM RECORD AY JUAREZ STAKE, CHIHUAHUA, MEXICO

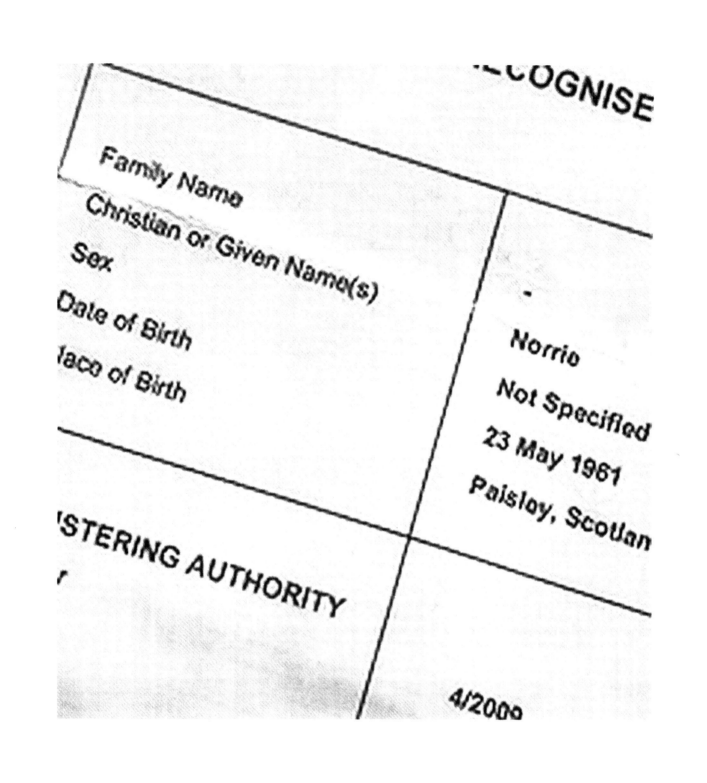

(24) "SEX NOT SPECIFIED" BIRTH CERTIFICATE
(Australia)

83

STATE OF CALIFORNIA
CERTIFICATION OF VITAL RECORD

STATE OF CALIFORNIA
DEPARTMENT OF PUBLIC HEALTH

CERTIFICATE OF LIVE BIRTH
STATE OF CALIFORNIA
USE BLACK INK ONLY

6A. LAST NAME	6B. MIDDLE NAME	6C. FIRST NAME	6D. RELATION TO CHILD ☐ MOTHER ☐ FATHER ☐ PARENT
9A. LAST NAME	9B. MIDDLE NAME	9C. FIRST NAME	9D. RELATION TO CHILD ☐ MOTHER ☐ FATHER ☐ PARENT

(25) "NO GENDER" OF (LGBT) PARENTS BIRTH CERTIFICATE
(California)

Little Girl in Florida Officially Has 3 Parents on Her Birth Certificate

By Lisa Sanchez, Reuters, February 8, 2013

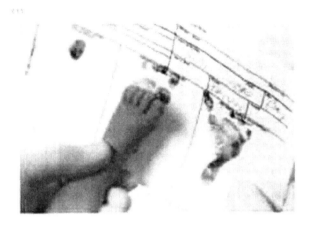

...A judge in Florida has approved that a 22-month-old baby girl will have all three of her parents on her birth certificate, a married lesbian couple and a gay man. This is all after a two-year paternity battle between the couple and their friend who donated his sperm but then wanted a larger role in the baby girl's life. The birth certificate will now include the names of the biological father and both women as parents. It's a bit of an unusual arrangement, but it's all been approved by the Miami-Dade Circuit Court Judge. Unfortunately, it seems that the modern family isn't all as happy as they could be since the 3-parent arrangement wasn't exactly what the mothers had in mind. Their attorney, Kenneth Kaplan, explained to Reuters:

> When push came to shove, they figured he would understand the situation. The mistake they made, however, was there should have been a written document spelling out what his rights and responsibilities were going to be.

Although getting this family together was a little tricky, the two moms now believe that they are doing the right thing because they "want Emma to have it all" and believe that including her biological father in some family outings will be in her best interests. In the end, it's all about family love, isn't it? One of the mommies, Cher Filippazzo, says that they "believe the best interest for Emma is for him to have a role in her life."

(26) 3 PARENT (LGBT) BIRTH CERTIFICATE
(Florida)

CPSIA information can be obtained at www.ICGtesting.com
Printed in the USA
BVOW04s1457260415

397673BV00005B/72/P